POETRY NOW NORTHERN ENGLAND 2002

Edited by

Heather Killingray

First published in Great Britain in 2002 by
POETRY NOW
Remus House,
Coltsfoot Drive,
Peterborough, PE2 9JX
Telephone (01733) 898101
Fax (01733) 313524

HB ISBN 0 75432 736 1
SB ISBN 0 75432 737 X

FOREWORD

Although we are a nation of poets we are accused of not reading poetry, or buying poetry books. After many years of listening to the incessant gripes of poetry publishers, I can only assume that the books they publish, in general, are books that most people do not want to read.

Poetry should not be obscure, introverted, and as cryptic as a crossword puzzle: it is the poet's duty to reach out and embrace the world.

The world owes the poet nothing and we should not be expected to dig and delve into a rambling discourse searching for some inner meaning.

The reason we write poetry (and almost all of us do) is because we want to communicate: an ideal; an idea; or a specific feeling. Poetry is as essential in communication, as a letter; a radio; a telephone, and the main criterion for selecting the poems in this anthology is very simple: they communicate.

CONTENTS

THE GOLF WIDOW

She absorbed the loss unto herself -
She possessed him in a new way -
Took his life - his cross -
Took an interest in gardening -
She would sit reminiscing
With the thought of him with her.
His angers turned her own like black clouds
There were petty quarrels - so she was never alone.

Sleeping, she saw him putt the ball
And as each ball landed she feared he would lose the game -
She knew his state of health
And advised him to give up the game -
She feared he would fall through too much exertion -
He had a heart complaint -
He died whilst playing his last game.

She treasured his golf clubs in memory
Received condolences from the Club -
So many of his friends did stand the loss.
She bought a seat and had his name engraved
And she placed it near the links -
In sad remembrance of him whilst playing his last game
She sat a while and cried - because he died!

M E Smith

HAPPY HOLIDAY

How really wonderful it is
To see the sky so blue.
The clouds have gone
The rain has stopped
And all because of you.
A lifting of the heart occurs
Depression fades away.
Each day is filled with happiness
Because you're here to stay
If only for a little while
The main thing I enjoy
Is cooking meals and feeding you.
You're Grandma's favourite boy.
We'll have some games together
And go into the park.
While you are playing football
I'll listen to the lark.
The song it sings has meaning,
It's saying 'Happiness
Is spending time together
Which relieves us of all stress.'
The pleasure of your company
Is more than I can say.
There's nothing better than delight
In this our holiday.

J Jones

TO BARBARA

We shed a tear when a friend dies,
Before spring came she closed her eyes,
Sudden on the morning the news is relayed
Flowers for Barbara and prayers are prayed.

We shed a tear when a friend dies,
The flowers all weep and the sun cries
A subtle posy sprinkled with dew
For a friend far away, a face that we knew.

Communication to remember a friend
We send her these snowdrops to the world's end,
A garland of rosebuds and violets for love,
A poem for Barbara in heaven above.

Jean Carroll

At Last

Spider like it crept
Silk spun threads
Shafts of darted light,
Briefly resting on the
Pillowed head, it sought
to pierce my sight.
Then out of the blue
But right on cue
Radio Four beamed forth.
Prayer for the day now
Underway, as wavelengths
Of vision returned,
Anecdotes quoted
Were duly noted
My new retired head
At its best.
On world events
Local news, I could
Linger and muse
Write to my hearts
Content.
Raising my arm
With my fist
In the air
I declared,
A definitive
Yes! Yes! Yes!

Edna Sarsfield

SHADOWS

These ubiquitous, soulless things don't eat, nor breathe, nor blink,
But seem to have eyes in the backs of their heads and the
calibre to think.
For their furtiveness allows them to trace every move you make.
But you're safe from these pretentious things when the world's awake.
There will always be one that will stick to you like glue.
It seeks pleasure in hiding and changes appearance like humans do.
Their intrinsic deceitfulness allows them by day to never scare
But when the sun sets and lights fades, they change
and you must beware.
It's at night their work begins and they awake from the dead,
When you're alone, shivering with fright, trying to sleep in your bed.
They surround you so that there's nowhere for you to escape.
If you're grabbed no one will hear your cries through its black,
velvet cape.
They tease, torment and taunt you to make you quake with fear,
Their ominous bodies are obscured except for a distinctive sneer.
Some of them relish lingering about in the darkness of the night
And often help to conceal an evil being from their victim's sight
So that not a soul will know of the murderer's identity
And the victim's loved ones have to live with grief for eternity.
For us fortunate ones, the nightmare ends when the cock starts to crow,
When the light strangles darkness and the devilish shadows all go . . .
That is until the sun sets again at the end of the day
And the shadows turn heinous and come out to play.

Alison Smullen (14)

THE SEASIDE DONKEY

I stand remembering days gone by now I have grown so old,
I've a tree to shade me from the sun, a shelter when it's cold.
In my buttercupped and daisied field I never feel alone
With bees and butterflies and birds I'm seldom on my own.
There's a friendly spider living in the bark of my big tree
Sometimes I have a talk with him - and he has a talk with me!
I ask him how he weaves his web, such a delicate fine skein
Which shines and sparkles in morning dew or when
                                    we've had some rain.
I remember sunshine, golden sands, small waves upon the sea,
The children paid their sixpences to have a ride on me.
A child unused to animals might approach me with some fear
Rub a small hand up my bristly mane and gently stoke my ear,
And how, sometimes, the bigger boys would laugh, and with a smile
Whisper to me in my ear, 'Please, would you gallop for a while?'
I remember when the tide came in our long day's work was done
Tired, we walked three donkeys to a row, as we jingle-jangled home.
A bag of oats, a long long drink and when the morning came
We were ready, eager, happy to go down to the sands again.
My coat was thick and furry, my hooves were strong and shiny black
I'd a dark cross shoulder to shoulder and down my sturdy back.
Now I think of all those happy years with the children on the shore
These days I leave that to the young ones, I don't go there anymore.
My owner brings me crunchy carrots, a bale of sweet fresh hay,
To quench my thirst, a bath of water which he refills every day.
Now I'm old and standing patiently in the shadow of my tree.
I think of Christ, Our Saviour, who rode a creature
                                    Just like me.

Pam Quigley

I SHOULD HAVE SAID I LOVE YOU

Although I loved you very much
I rarely told you so
I felt it wasn't necessary
It was something you would know
So why do I feel guilty
Now that you're not here
Why didn't I just say
'I love you so, my dear.'
If I could have you back again
I'd tell you every day
But this will never happen
No matter how I pray
I'm sorry I never told you
Throughout our many years
But now I tell you every day
Whilst silently shedding tears.

J Gilchrist

HEIKE

A blond bombshell
Exploding in freefall
From marriage blues;
On tour to St Petersburg
And Liverpool.
A Jehovah gypsy
In Beatle clothes,
Giving her love
To just men
On the road.
A super-lamb-banana queen,
A damsel d'Hamburg
Photographing an artist's dreams.

A love due
For the next century,
Hanging out
Of the gardens of Babylon
With each witnessed track,
Guides to another heaven
And as such, never looking back.

Peter Corbett

WIND

I hear the wind
Blow through the trees
And it startles me.

For the wind that I hear
Blowing through the trees
Heavy with their summer leaves
Causes the loud hissing sigh.

This sigh is like a sea's sigh
Heard on returning tides,
And yet I hear it now
On leaf and bough.

The boughs sway,
And the leaves tremble,
Yet they do not fall,
For this year is not yet old.

But the leaves will fall,
They will age and die,
And the wind will blow again,
And gather them up.

For the wind blows where it will,
And I hear the sound of it,
And notice the trees,
And the affect upon myself.

Robert Lockett

IN LIFE WHAT ARE WE EXPECTING?

Firstly we want good health and security.

Then as we grow older we
expect marriage and children
also,
Love, respect, kindness
And above all tolerance and luck
A lot of these things are
Gained only by our own
Living and efforts.

J Campbell Jones

LOST CHILD

There's a certain magic in the woods
That's why we all play there
Parents sit on benches and wait
For the children to return
Remembering not so long ago
When they once ran in there.

The bogeyman will get ya
The playful child is warmed
As the woods get darker
It's time to head for home
While one mother she still sits
So cold and very alone.

None of the children play there now
Since they lost their friend
A bogeyman or something worse
Took their friend away
That certain magic that filled the wood
Has melted fast away.

Rodger Moir

DRAGGING MOMENTS

Footfalls in the depth of night
Arise me from my sleep
They sound as if they have boots on
With chains around their feet
I hear the dragging moments
Of the chains along the floor
So sorrowful and vacant
Are their footfalls once more
One wishes that one could really help
But perhaps help is on its way
So just for now I will eradicate
And then turn again to pray
Of the passing of the footfalls
With chains around their feet
So sorrowful and vacant
Which aroused me from my sleep.

A E Jones

SUMMER DAYS

The warm breeze against the heated sun
With the start of a summer's day begun.
Strolling across the field and up the hill
Breathing the scented air, and all is still.
Listening to the chattering birds around,
The cuckoo in the distance, Heaven most profound
Hedges thick with yellow broom and sweet
And summer roses at one's feet.
A butterfly fluttering past, a child at play.
Enjoying the long hot summer's day.
The hum of a solitary bee passing by
Not a cloud in sight, within the deep blue sky.
Peace, perfect peace, and God has claimed his own
The world is all his, and glory is the crown.

R P Candlish

A GENTLE YIELDING

A cat's timid jouncing footprints
Through the snow
Had beckoned my own ice-crunching step
To up and follow

Through the churchyard graves, deep drifts,
Black bone eaves,
While my steaming breath screamed 'Life! Life!'
To all the unborn leaves.

The doe-like snowy pads led on,
Some ballet divine
Etched in the thick glistering velvety fall
By that furtive feline.

Where her clandestine ramblings did wend,
I was not to know;
Honour, with twisted root and grave, whispered
'Yield,' through snow.

For all I knew, those secret elven pads
Holly bound, away,
Could have melted in some summer realm
Where ever the cats will play.

Seán Rooney

MAY LOVE BECOME MY DESTINY

I'm all alone
In this soulless world
Left stranded in every moment I've grieved
Betrayed by faith
Hounded by pain
Spurned by the one I believed

My world became a total eclipse
Barren of all sentiment and love
My world just haemorrhages silence
Introducing tears where laughter once stood

Am I to blame
Am I but cursed
Does guilt possess this terrible revenge
But in a while
I must renounce
This treason my heart must avenge

Love had left my social realm
Running from the dream in my heart
Abandoning a vow lit in my soul
Leaving my world in the dark

I journey moods
I search my mind
I send prayers to negotiate peace
I scramble round
To touch belief
Hoping this nightmare will cease

I must pray to save my world
To flower the dreams I propose
Thus may love become my destiny
And my heart meets with its rose

David Bridgewater

WEDDING VOWS

When you take your wedding vows,
- For better or for worse,
Make sure you really mean them,
Or you might as well be cursed.

Will you really love this partner,
- For your whole entire life?
If not then you must not become,
- A husband or a wife.

For richer or for poorer,
You'll be poorer - more than rich,
If you really cannot stand this thought,
- It's no good getting hitched.

In sickness and in health is next,
- They can't get out of bed,
If you've considered all these things,
Then go ahead, - get wed.

Joyce Clegg

MORNING WALK

I saw a ship sailing in a cloud today.
Water deep, air clear, birds in song.
People walk in silent contemplation
of dreams and realities that cloud their way.
Dogs bark in demanding tones, traffic hurries air
that had done no wrong.
Buildings stagger against the age of the world.
Dust gathers in graveyard heaps marking passing progress.
Skies part to open for jet people on their way.
I saw a ship sailing in a cloud today.

D N Grufferty

GARDEN MEMORIES

Browsing in the garden on a sunny afternoon
Memories come drifting back of nearly every shrub and bloom,
Laurel and the ivy and the graceful buddleia,
Honeysuckle and hearts tongue fern make their appearance every year.
Mock orange blossom, in full bloom shedding petals along the way
Cydonia and forsythia too, have so many things to say.

We have a Virginia creeper climbing over the garden shed,
Young tendrils waving in the breeze, first green then turns to red.
It takes me back to a place I knew, standing in well-kept grounds
Surrounded by fields and woodland, and wildlife could be found,
Where we spent so many happy hours just roaming I recall
And the Virginia creeper grew and grew, and covered the building wall.

Wild violets lurked neath shady trees, and blue hyacinths you could see
We picked raspberries in season, and had fresh fruit tart for tea.
Maybe if we wandered up the stream there would be watercress about,
And if we were very quiet, perhaps we'd see a trout.
Brambles too in season were prolific at their height
And for weeks the large preserving pan was seldom out of sight.

So, though our Virginia creeper sometimes gets in the way,
It is part of a store of memories, that will always with me stay.

Elsie Mather

THE KEY

The key is turned on the dockyard gate,
Sealing forever, shipbuilding's fate,
See the iron drag chains, covered in mould and rust,
Lying on the slipway covered in dust,
The scrap man calls and collects the best,
Leaving the hungry seagulls, to scavenge the rest,
The final launch is done, the vessel departs,
Leaving the redundant workers with saddened hearts,
For the key is turned on the dockyard gate,
Sealing forever, shipbuilding's fate.

The huge test bed is silent,
Its running, at last ceased,
The giant ship engine gone, along with the bronze threepenny piece,
Which, during the test run, stood on its edge,
For during the weeks the engine was running,
Never once, did that coin fall down,
Such was the precision, and the engineering,
The crankshafts, fore and aft, and the exact steering.
While the shipyard closure drew ever nearer,
Now the workshops are empty, gone the electrician and fitter's mate,
And that key is now turned forever, on the shipyard gate . . .

Gordon Bannister

THE DREAM

I dreamed death came to me last night
Heaven's gates opened wide
An angel of the Lord came by
And ushered me inside.

There to my astonishment
Stood folk I'd known on Earth
Those whom I'd judged as most unfit
And to be of little worth

But when I walked amongst them
Guess what I did see?
Every face showed stunned surprise
For no one expected me.

E B Dawes

JUST LIFE
(Dedicated to the memory of Beatrice Lillian)

She sits, head bowed,
Thoughts twisting and turning,
Memories drift in and out,
Lazy, shapeless,
Time passed, missed, lost.
Sharing secret smiles, past loves.
Tears for the ones she's lost,
Wishing she were gone
Not left to grow old,
Lonely, slowly, wasting away,
Every day a torture,
Long, endless, leading to one more,
Why her, why is she left
The only survivor
Not of some war,
Just life . . .?

Jane Stallwood

BELOVED

My life blood flows.
Surgeon's knife is wielded with precision
as I be a lamb to be slaughtered.
Love my parents gave pulled me through.
It didn't work for them: My love is not strong.
I haven't been alive long enough yet to comprehend the
meaning to be loved and loved back in return.

Barry Welburn

BUSINESS INTERRUPTED

Suddenly there may come uncalled,
Gatecrashing in upon licensed thoughts,
Routinely rewarded for their channelled flow
Their consistent issue as a printed strip
Unreeled from a roller within the mind, -

Sweeter thoughts, like rosebuds strung
By a past, persistent childish hand
Upon the steel frame of adult toil,
Or as daisy-chains to loop among office wires.

Though so often are these lost, like wisps of hay
Caught on a hedge, soon again blown off,
Such chance intrusions at times gain a hold:
Unemotionally we are functioning, automatically reacting,
Churning as monotonously as a cement mixer chews its cud
The impressions the printed page has applied, -

Then the breeze wafts in a faint scent from afar
And the live thing within us, within the machine,
Responds with a flood of secretion, - with the effect
Of a fallen bough on to the supply lines:
The current flickers and the fuses, blow,
The machine summed up by the treacly flow
From the hidden, the dormant natural self;
And a river of memory or unrestrained feeling
Roars over the site where the mill had stood.

Margaret Mawston

TO MY WIFE

There comes a time in every man's life,
When he needs to take himself a wife,
I met a beauty, that beauty was you,
An hourglass figure and red hair too.
A shy charming smile, eyes turned to the ground
I just couldn't believe,
What a treasure I'd found.
A ready-made family of three plus one
And that marvellous girl barely twenty-one.
We had our troubles as we went through life
But was made a lot sweeter,
With you as my wife.
And as we go through our remaining years,
I close my eyes to suppress the tears,
And as I'm lying in my bed,
Once again I can picture
That hair so red, those big brown eyes
That shy charming smile,
And thank God that he sent you,
To me for a while.
It's forty years since you took my hand,
They joined us together,
I gave you a band.
There's not much left to say now
That we're over the hill,
But to say that I love you
And I always will.

Fred Wallis

AGE OF TIME

The future's unknown to us
But one thing's for sure
We're all getting old
And there's no cure.

The days spent lazing in the haze shall fade
As time goes by like a plane
People change, people grow
Most we never know.

As the cracks begin to show
We realise were getting old
Grey and wrinkled we become
Inside were all still young
We don't want to look at what we have become

The age is now showing
The final curtain is so near
As we try to figure out why
Life is not so clear.

D Lissamore

THIEF IN THE NIGHT

On goes the hat and pull on the gloves
This lad's a rebel cos it's twocking he loves
Scarf round the mouth and tracky zipped up
Cos if twocking's a game he'll lift the cup
He says he's the master and the master he is
Everyone's seen him; they say he's the biz!
Think of a car he's burnt it out
100 cars easy! Of which there's no doubt
If it's a cozzy he's after, a cozzy he'll get
If you don't believe him he'll start taking bets
This boy's on a mission, a thief in the night
If he sees the rozzas he's out of sight
He spies a nice Audi but he's had six before
The cozzy's the best, he knows the score
His luck's in tonight he sees one pull up
The driver gets out, he's getting stitched up
He's up on his toes with a click of his heels
He can't wait to start bezzin' about in these wheels
Pop goes the door lock, steering lock broken
Here comes the geezer you gotta be jokin'
Out comes the screwy and give it a twist
The engine roars loudly this bloke must be p****d
He pops a 180 cos he slammed in reverse
This boy's a genius things can't get much worse
He leaves the scene of the crime with no cares on his mind
This boy is happy cos these are so hard to find
He starts his show with a handbreak or two
Maybe a doughnut, he knows what to do
All his mates cheer as they watch his show
He's the best driver and everyone knows
Then out of nowhere he sees some blue lights
This is a shock it's gonna be tight
Cool as a cucumber, don't start to flap
Here comes a junction and he sees a gap
'Laters! Bobbies you ain't catching me!'
This is his cry, as he starts to flee

He's sweating like mad as he dumps the car
He's got to be quick the police can't be far
Quick as a flash he sets it alight
He won't be caught cos he's off in the night
Another car nicked and screwdriver in hand
He'll make this world into a twockers wonderland.

S J Wilson

A TEAR

What is this falling like a raindrop on glass,
This globe of compassion, this jewel so clear,
Full to the brim with all the sadness,
Flowing with sorrow, love and fear.
The music throbbed and trembled,
From deep within the soul it is felt,
Reflecting hurt and suffering,
The hardest heart it would melt.
All the heartache, all the anger,
Linked vibrations of pure sound,
The light shows a glistening tear,
As it slowly, slowly, meanders down.

K Ainsley

INCANDESCENT MOON

You are,
    My treasure
As in my arms,
        Your body slips
And I kiss away,
            The moisture
From your,
    Sweet lips.
To hear
    The fields of barley
Ripple,
    As the gentle air
With its warm summer breath,
            Scented
By the hawthorn and honeysuckle
                Envelops,
The warm summer night.

The long,
    Soft grass,
            Between our toes
Then,
    The cool running water,
                of the stream
Splashing over our feet.
                The rustle
Of the leaves
            From the warm
Nigh breeze
        Faint echoes
Of a familiar tune
            Under the incandescent moon.

C F Hauxwell

A BIRTH OF HE

A well-known man of long ago,
he spoke his words and shared
with you, Rabbie Burns of he
you know, of Scotland for here
he goes. For he has told the
times of that has passed by,
for through his words there was
a cry, a cry of spoken tales of
through his days, for hear him
now, but he has gone away.
A death of a man, of that he was
proud, for within your hearts, he
is still around.
You hear his name of Scotland he
be, for the birth of this child of
hope but he sees.
To leave your mark, for when you
are gone, the time to take, it will
not be long.
Because of words, of that come from
he, for no one bothered but he could
see, the life and times of this man
he.

Shauna Hamilton

WILDERNESS

When I look back on our love
I see ghosts of hectic wandering
In lands of desire, lust and confusion . . .

The cuckoo cried out from the top-field;
'Fools, fools . . .'

In the field below,
I saw you
Contemplating a spinning bicycle wheel.
Behind you the land was filled
with strange sculptures
Signifying your own history.
Half-evolved bodies, dried hollow in their death-throes.
Their hands pathetically grasping a useless Heaven.
Their legs dangle in a disturbed peace,
Facial masks of sad, happy and nonchalant expressions
Are aligned to flowering shrubs
And of course,
Dead trees.

Just add water I thought.

The stale Summer air pervades everything
With a dormant expectancy

The dream encounters a door to reality
And stops dead.

M P Smith

SPRING

Ho! to see the snowdrop
Crocus and daffodil
Bursting from the frozen earth
The ghastly winter to kill
And watch again the swallows
The martins and the swifts
To marvel at their antics
One of nature's loving gifts
To bring forth again the springtime
The birds to nest and sing
Hooray! it's getting warm again
Suddenly it is spring.

Ted Gutridge

RHYME AND REASON

Poetry in motion
Such a lovely thought
Poetry emotion
Passion leaves us wrought

Rhyming verse
Sounds so tranquil
Rhyming curse
Not so thankful

A 'jaunty' ditty
Makes you smile
But sometimes more gritty
May not then beguile

Nursery rhymes
Many a younger listener
But between the lines
Something more sinister

Many wartime writers
Depicted the war
But who were the fighters
Really fighting for

For rhyming, use reason
It will make you think
Well-hidden meanings
Make a bittersweet drink.

Karen Swan

OUR SATURDAY MATINEE

Local flea pit
Saturday morning
Bedlam of kids
Matinee dawning
Stampede of feet
Doors rattle open
Rush for a seat
Before they are taken
Gaslights dimmed
Flickering images
Smoking guns firing
Arrows flying
Thundering horses
Bugles sounding
Cavalry to the rescue
Cheering feet
Wagon train saved
Lovers meet
Interval ice cream
Cardboard tubs
Behaving like monkeys
Usherette's beam
Gaslights dimmed
Cheer of excitement
Captain Marvel
Hour of contentment
Gaslights full on
God Save The Queen
Out into the sunshine
To live it again.

Mel Bartliff

34

VIEW FROM A HILL

We laboured up that high incline
Collapsed on sandstone seat
And wondered at God's patchwork quilt
Spread out beneath our feet

Distant industrial dinosaurs
Stood stark against the sea
Below pastures green, brown and gold
Made a contrasting tapestry

To our left the backbone of the hills
Interspersed by moorland fell
Flowed down to meet the lushness
Of the land we know so well

Below a rambling caterpillar
Set out on sheep-worn path
The only sound that assailed its ears
Was the cry of pheasant wrath

High above on gaudy wings
The hang-gliders dipped and soared
And unperturbed, the skylark rose
Serenaded with song outpoured

Suddenly clouds parted
Sunlight hit the ground
Spreading its fiery fingers
To light the scene around

There before our very eyes
Earth and sky were meeting
And we knew in our hearts
It was God Himself we were greeting.

Sue Ireland

ONE MISSION

Now can you see how my soul has flown
Through time and space to enter the unknown.
Once a star shining so bright
Transformed by God into angelic light.
Entering the womb of a living Mother Earth
To clothe me in person ready for birth.
Then the day I was born to learn
The highs and lows of an emotional term.
New experiences each and every day
Growing up and always ready to play.
An eager baby and a happy child
Precocious teenager with a temper quite wild.
Then in an instant the adult did appear
Destined to travel with God always near.
Spreading my light to every sad soul
Wanting to heal and love is my goal.
Now with my true love always at my side
We spread the good word to all far and wide.
And I myself will soon be another
Who bring a little angel to accompany her brothers.
So the cycle from beginning to end
Light upon light with services to lend.
And soon the world will be overcome by light
To free all fears and abolish any fight.
What a sight it will be to behold
With harmony and love befriending all souls.
Living together with no reasons to fear
With the light of God's message oh so clear.
Always give what you want to receive
Then Heaven's peace on Earth is yours to conceive.

Karen Harrison

WAR

A man clutches his child, and desperately tries
To protect him from missiles, that rain down from the skies.
His cries for help are directed at passers by,
But they don't seem to help as they run on by.

Huddled in a doorway, father and son,
He clutches desperately, just keeps holding on,
Smoke appears and fills the sky
The figures disappear, father and child.

When the smoke clears, on the war-torn street,
The child he was holding falls to his feet,
Motionless and lifeless, he lays upon the floor,
The man who once held him, stares from the door.

Looking around as though asking for help,
He falls to his knees and lets out a yell,
Crying inconsolably, he asks why,
Why his son was the one to die?

A war of religion, fighting for good,
Two sides divided, and they worship the same God.
If they would worship together and stand hand in hand,
Then this world would change with peace across the land.

Andrew Brian Zipfell

SMOKING

Smoking, smoking, I can hear choking

It will ruin your health
And disintegrate your wealth.

Smoking, smoking, I can hear choking

You will lose all your friends
it is not in the trends

Smoking, smoking, I can hear choking

You will lose your breath
It can end in death.

Eleanor Clark

A NEW DIMENSION

It's over now, there is no pain
I'm floating in a starry space
My faculties are one again
I love the feeling of this place
Just when I thought it was the end
It proved to be a brand-new start
I only wish that I could send
Loved ones, the joy within my heart
For some day soon their souls will fly
Into this place of golden light
No clocks to tick as time goes by
And no such thing as day and night
It's such a pity we don't know
Whilst we draw our earthly breath
That from this level, when we go
There's no such thing as death.

Edward A Walker

THE END IS NIGH - OR IS IT A LIE?

Always keep the dream alive
Don't forget and it will survive
You can't let the memories ever die
Never listen to those who lie
Who pretend they're high
And say they won't die
Why do they lie
We all die
But do you ever wonder why
What does it mean the end is nigh
The lives we lead are just a lie
And the world we live in will one day die

We pretend Heaven's the sky
We'll be there wondering why
Starting to cry
Trying to deny
Laughing at the days gone by
Just remember back and wonder why
Why, why do we all die
Is it fixed the wrong's passed by
Or is it that we all survive
Whatever you do don't spread the lie
Just to yourself you can ask why
Am I the one who will survive

What is this thing called déjà vu
And is this thing a part of you
At the back of my mind I know what is true

I just can't see me getting old
I'm not being big or either bold
Because of this voice which I have been told
That I'm going to die young
I will die before my life's begun
So to this I implore
As I have got to say more

For I have seen the day I die
Cause God he flew me up to the sky
And showed me the plot where I will lie

But why does it only follow me
Who's is this voice only I can see
If it's my creator then so let it be.

Christopher Heslop

OLD AGE

Silent they sit there, the lost and lonely ones
Longings, like hunger, unappeased
Save for the familiarity of daily bread.
Expectation a condition scarce to be remembered.
The day near ended eyes and ears
Are ready to receive the whispers which spell life
The cooling, creaking timbers, fall of ash in the grate.
The old dog, snuffling and snorting
Reliving scents and sounds in dusty dreams.
The clock monotony reassuring.
Soft rain taps on the window,
Reminder of the world outside.
All listened for, garnered and held precious
Against the hours of night.
All credits counted, save for tomorrow's balance
Leaving a grain of living still in hand,
Hoarded and unspent to greet them with the dawn
When sound and sight meets sleep slow overtaking
Even memories like a tree's last leaves
Strip them one by one and leave them bare.
Their spring lies underground
And winter glances back no more
To the green leaves of the past.

Marjorie Copleston

YOU DON'T UNDERSTAND

You pass us in the street
(My son and me).
You think I'm a bad mother
But you really do not see.
My son has temper tantrums
He screams and shouts a lot.
You see me as a failure
But it's not my fault. It's not.
If he was mine, I'd smack him
You say behind my back.
So let me tell you something
You're all well off the track.
My son, you see, has autism
He's not like you and I,
You think I don't control him
But believe you me, I try.
He questions who, what, why and when
Every single day.
He doesn't understand
Why he can't go out and play.
So remember this poem
When you see me about.
My son is autistic
My son's not a lout.

Andrea Henderson

HOLY ISLAND

Here are the bridges
Built by man,
Spanning the Tyne
Gateway
Both day and night
To a Northern Kingdon
Unrivalled Celtic wisdom,
The silence of eternity
Speaks,
Infiltrates our world,
Fortifies friend and stranger
On the sacred island
Lindisfarne,
Windswept, tidal,
Medicinal air
Magnet for visitors
Searching,
Seeking freedom from
Brooding chaos
In contemporary living,
Bemused,
Finding self
Following the footsteps
Of silence seekers,
Saints
Encompassing the waters,
Life's tide turning
Renewing vision
Relationships,
On the Holy Island
Lindisfarne.

Nora M Davidson

AUTUMN

Oh Autumn, why do you have to join
In the dance of Summer's death?
Your cool, cool air makes flowers fade
And greens all turn to gray.
Your light is bright
But has no warmth
You lift the sun too high.
Roses lose their perfume
Their petals droop, sadly browned
As leaves fall into water,
All are drowned
Their bared arms implore the return of nature's cloak.

Soon you will sleep Autumn,
Your bric-a-brac will fade, be buried
Under Winter's cold glittering array
Of snow-drenched pastures.
Lambs and ladies in shiny boots
Will slip and slide through a dangerous youth,
While you oh Autumn
Nestled in sleep,
Care not for the old, infirm, the weak;
Would that you could dance through Winter's song
And leave us our laughter
In an eternal summer sun.

Joanna Parry

THE PILGRIMAGE

They come on differing journeys,
the pilgrims, travelling here;
they come on foot, by rail, and road,
or, from further afield, by air;
they come on different pilgrimages,
carrying many and varied loads

Some come the scenery to view,
by creation's hand to be renewed;
to find in land, and sea, and bird
a solace for their lives, now undeterred
by pressure and by time, to find
that peace which is Divine.

Some come to follow in the steps
which long ago, the saints once trod,
to find in ancient stone and sod
a lingering holiness and peace,
which down the centuries have never
ceased to renew and enfold.

Others come in silence to be still,
to find from deep within, the Saviour's will;
to seek in study and in prayer, and, in
the stillness, to meet Him there;
to be wrapped in swaddling bands of love,
healed by the spilling of His blood.

What e'er their needs when they come
to this place
all are gifted by His grace.

Catherine Riley

A LETTER FROM AMERICA

One day William H Ducker sailed to a far distant land.
A father, a mother, two children at hand,
To make their mark on a country so new,
So brave of heart, but they were so few,
And as the time rolled slowly by
This stalwart band began to multiply,
They gave us a family we never knew we had
Born from the children of that mother and dad
Who were lost to us - through time and space
Just distant names without a trace:
Till one day - just out of the blue
The postman brought us news of you.
News of the family we didn't know we had
Born from that early mum and dad.
It gave us great joy, and we shed a tear
Your letter from America has brought you so near,
But this I must say, maybe I'm a bit bold
Welcome all you Duckers young and old.
Let us keep a hold of this very old name,
Never let our families be lost to each other again
And let us band together, to find out our past
Because of this effort our future will last.
Photographs and letters that's all we need
To put faces and names to this hardy breed.
So through this poem Jane I hope you understand,
Stay safe, and may God hold you all in the palm of His hand . . .

Brian Ducker

WHEN THE WORD WAS SAID

When I first said the word 'Mum'
it was a long time ago
how often have I said it since
that would be good to know

But I know her prayers were simple
'The war should end,' she said 'and thus
with God's help we'll build a world
a peaceful one for all of us . . .'

There was though a question in life
which she hardly understood:
Why's so much evil on Earth
when most of the people are good?

Her prayers had no reply,
she left the world as it stood:
in conflict that still remains
between the evil and the good.

Anthony Gyimes

HOLIDAYS

Holidays are great times for leisure
We look forward to them with pleasure
Some may stay at home without the fuss
Maybe visit a castle using a local bus.
Could be foreign resorts we like
But watch out for a sudden strike.
Who wants to spend time at an airport
That was not really what we sought.
The heat intense, one can hardly breathe,
Please give us air and room for ease.
But all is forgotten when you arrive at the pool
Isn't it nice having a dip and feeling cool.
The food may cause a tummy upset
But not to worry if that's all you get
Returning home, it's here comes the rain
Do you wish to be back in Spain again.
But isn't there something to be said
For sleeping in your own comfortable bed.
Wake up in the morning to a nice cup of tea
Everything just as it should be.
Next year's holiday looms ahead today
So how will we respond I wouldn't like to say
Most likely it will rest on what we have to pay
But put worries behind you and enjoy the holiday.

Eleanor Alderson

THE FOSTERING

I am your mother, I chose you from the start -
From out raw mingling of
Waste and ravages of
Disease, where, in the ripe
Noon's glaring the harshly
Cackling carrion crows
Advanced, near-sated on
The final dross of war.

Does it matter that I
Am white and you are black?
I know all I lack is
Held in your small hands.

Margret Phillips

LOVER'S TIFF

Dim the lights, let music play,
Drowning sorrows of the night,
Calming the soul at the end of day.

No more words. No more to say.
Too tired to continue with the fight.
Dim the lights, let music play.

Gentle sounds soothe fears away,
Prompting the question who was right.
Calming the soul at the end of day.

Head bowed, eyes closed in prayer.
Looking for answers before daylight.
Dim the lights, let music play.

Blackened mood turning to grey.
Blue horizons somewhere in sight,
Calming the soul at the end of day.

Differences resolved come what may.
Tomorrow maybe we just might,
Dim the lights, let music play,
Calming the soul at the end of day.

Joy Miller

NOT A PROBLEM

As I walk along an empty beach,
The cathedral bells just out or reach.
I find a dry and inviting rock,
And sit and listen to the cathedral clock.
As I sit my feet sink into the sand,
And I sit and sit with my head in my hands.
Then I look up to the cloud-streaked sky,
Thinking to myself, why - oh - why.
So I let my mind drift like the sea,
Wondering why problems come to me.
Then I feel better because of a chilling breeze,
But start to walk before I freeze.
And I let my imagination roam,
Relaxing on my slow walk home.
Once I am home I lie upon my bed,
Tossing my troubles around in my head.
And listening to my own heartbeat,
And my next-door neighbour's stomping feet.
And now I relax because my mind is free,
It was not really a problem for me.

Rab Melvin

TYNE SUPREME

Our coaly Tyne, they used to boast
was 'Queen of a'al the rivers',
but for a child, it drove you wild,
for rats gave you the shivers.

Yet join us now and feel our pride;
you'll surely be amazed
at architectural splendour,
with dereliction all erased.

There may well be a dearth of ships,
but the *in place* is right here,
with dancing, food and lots of fun,
not forgetting the beer.

As for the view from every bridge,
we're now a film-maker's dream,
for variety in every span
makes our River Tyne supreme.

Cynthia Smith

LADY LUCK

I've done the pools for years and years
And never won a groat,
While some have won repeatedly,
Which really gets my goat.

It's not as tho' I'm greedy -
A modest sum would do;
A little bit to play with;
An extra quid or two.

The folk who scoop a fortune
Can afford to make a splash.
I'd settle for a ripple
With that extra bit of cash.

When Lady Luck is smiling,
She never seems to see
That the person looking hopeful,
Is hard up little me!

If she only put her specs on,
I'm sure she'd realise
That the person looking hopeful
Is overdue a prize.

Dear Lady Luck, I'm asking
Will you try to smile on me,
And If I cannot win the pools,
Can I win the Lottery?

Vivian Finlay

IN FORTY YEARS' TIME
(To PW)

How will we be in forty years' time?
When you're 97 and I'm 96?
Will we still be writing in rhyme
And keep getting up to all our old tricks?

How, by then, will your blood pressure be
And what of the phlegm on my chest?
Will we both still be able to see
And walk without taking a rest?

The music we play and the people we meet
Will they be the same as today?
Will we still share or love as we sit down to eat
And feel we're so close when we pray?

Only God knows the truth of what is in store
For lovers who trust in His grace;
In the end we're united in Him evermore
Hearts on fire by the light of His face.

Anthony Manville

PEACE AND GOODWILL

It's time to celebrate the birth,
Of the greatest man, who lived on earth.
He changed our lives, through his behaviour,
The Son of God, who became our saviour.
He was so gentle, kind and good,
Though we were weak, he understood.
Always forgiving our every misdeed.
Saying a prayer, for our spiritual need.
As this special day comes around again.
Joy, goodwill and peace to all men.

Audrey Walker

THE COUNTRY

Sit under a tree, out in the country,
and see what I see
it's better than TV.

On the river bank, see a dragonfly,
hear a splash in the river nearby,
as a trout catches a fly.

And in the distant summer sky,
you'll hear the crow's cry,
and the flapping of wings and
other birds fly by.

You'll see the colour of the flowers
and the shades of green, in among the trees
and catch the fragrance,
on the summer breeze.

And at the end of the day, when you walk away,
relaxed and at one with the country,
I think you'll agree with me
it's better than TV.

Karl Garrett

PICTURED IN THE SKY

Earth's multicoloured canopy
The ever-changing sky
That seems to stretch out endlessly
Perhaps where angels fly
Indeed a mighty canvas spread
A constant picture show
Diverse in beauty, often said
By those who watch below
The moving sky, much can reveal
Strange citadels and trees
Strong images that look so real
Of distant lands and seas
Where, after storms, and grey clouds flee
A turquoise quilt unfolds
With sunbeams dancing merrily
In dappled shades of gold
As night's dark velvet cloak drops down
And twinkling stars delight
Rising moon's celestial gown
On Earth and sky shines bright
We view 'the heavens' constantly
Where hidden wonders lie
Enthralled each time we look and see
Those pictures in the sky!

Patricia Whittle

THE 5TH OF NOVEMBER

Remember, remember the 5th of November,
Always remember your firework code,
Stand back and watch them safely explode.
Watch the rocket light up the sky,
And wonder how far it will go, how high?
How much did you make for penny for the guy?
Tiny fragments that sparkle like stars,
That can travel many miles afar.
Watch that Catherine Wheel spin around,
See the bonfire burn to the ground.
Hold that sparkler in your hand,
The 5th of November can be just grand.
Bang, whoosh, whizz, the sound they make,
Be careful, as some of them could be fakes.
Always keep them in a cool dry place,
Otherwise they could injure the human or animal race.
Always light them from a distance,
As they could go off and knock you into another existence.
Make the 5th of November an enjoyable night,
Without giving anyone a fright.

Tina Rooney

PENSIVE THOUGHTS

In melancholy mood he ponders
relevance of earthly existence.
In cavernous mind, he disbelieves that
death is an ultimate ending,
when the body husk concludes.

Maybe there is some after life,
where loved ones here again united
to renew joys of a previous being.
Possibly in this divine hereafter
concepts of love and body are opposed
to former understanding,
yet real and gratifying.

Alex Branthwaite

IT'S OVER

You don't have to tell me I already know,
There's no more attention like there used to be.
You're wavering now it's starting to show,
Your life, it no more revolves around me.
Your ever decreasing words of romance
The look in your eye is now gone,
That gently touch, that fleeting glance
No more refer to us both being one.
It's failing now, so what do I do?
Without being hurt by rejection,
I'm holding on in the hope that you
Might return me some needed affection.
It's over now, I already know,
But you haven't the courage to tell me to go.

Kathleen Morris

FALLEN SNOW

The snow falls slowly, gentle and light,
Creating a carpet that's beautifully white.
Fluttering, flying and fleeing about,
Its presence creating excited shouts.

Minuscule flakes swirling round in a blizzard,
Changing the ground like a wicked, white wizard.
Each shape unique in its own special way,
Here for a moment or maybe a day.

Taking the shape of wherever it lands,
Then wrapping it up with firm cold hands.
Refusing to move, it freezes, still in one place,
Determined to be the object's new face.

Then, slowly but surely it disappears,
Knowing that there is no home for it here.
I look at the place where it once used to be.
I think of its beauty and smile happily.

Alex Marie Goldsmith (12)

BIRD SQUAWK

Morning in the north-east screeches on the ear
as, in from the North Sea comes birds,
the smaller birds all fear.

Their huge white breasts puff out as they
strut across the lawn,
the bouncers of the bird world who think
for them, grass was mown.

They spread great white wings like a lady
opening her fan,
while pigeons back off like an army beating
their retreat, how fast they ran.

A child holding ice cream cones in his hand,
is wondering where they have gone, but
takes it rather bland.

No wonder once that they thought a sailor's soul,
flew out amongst the seagulls rather than
become a ghoul.

The freedom of the sky and of the ground.
It should be the north's emblem as they seem
to move around.

Jean Paisley

YOU KNOW WHERE I LIVE

Two voices down the wire
Say different things to my soul
One message reaches me
One passed me by

Two voices down the wire
Push needing, very different buttons
One finds me at home
One found me out

Could it be the warmth of the stranger?
Reaches far deeper than she'll ever know
Could it be those seductive tones?
Ignite these feelings disturbing me below

Can't disclose the dilemmas inside
Everybody has choices to make
Can't tell her about the way it's become
Our geography is the saving of me

Two voices down the wire
Create images for now and for tomorrow
One shows me security
One brings tantalising danger

Two voices down the wire
Disturb my life's anticipated map
One tells me - 'Good night'
One said - 'You know where I live . . . '

Bernard Harry Reay

BECKONING THE MOMENT

I sea her like the ocean
Capacious with devotion,
With her vernal smile
And aestival eyes,
Her autumn hair,
She's winter wise,
A girl for all seasons,
With legs to heaven
Like a levin
Striking me
With harmony.
Under the tree
Where I long to whisper,
Beneath the shade,
That may pervade
To permeate,
And dedicate,
Myself to that thirst kiss before the silence.

Anthony John Ward

LIGHT BEYOND THE SHADOWS

A foolish heart
pumping its rhythm
a singing sea
mourning its short life
a running shadow
seeking its soul

A vision alive
within the breaking sanity
words given to those
who live without hope
words that can mend
words that can give
a new dawn

Light trickles
from the poisoning dark
a gap for hope appears
words spoken with truth
lift forever the spirit
words woven together
telling us
unity is the way forward.

Gary Theys

THE NEGLECTED HOME OF THE DEAD?

Mist rolling over the erected slabs
Wind howling through the six-foot grass
Rain droplets trickling down the
Once shining angels made of brass
The neglected home of the dead?

Beds of newspaper stained with gin
Smashed photos of smiling faces
Rusting padlocks on unopened gates
Used needles with heroin traces
The neglected home of the dead?

Splintered glass along the eroded paths
Swirling, trampled grass bike tracks
Popped balls left without thought
Discarded gum along the grave backs
The neglected home of the dead?

Laughing youths with no respect
Stumbling on the few left stood
Falling down the half-dug plots
And vandalising those, which still look half good
The neglected home of the dead?

No more glorious sunny days
And no more relatives with daffodils in hand
No more fond memories revisited
And no more rituals to understand
Stripping the dead of their dignity
Not allowing the graves to stand proud
Forgetting the achievements made when alive
Smashing the pride, which once was loud
In the neglected home of the dead

Hollie Cheadle

WHISPER

Whisper, whisper in my ears, those sweet pretty words,
Whisper, whisper into my heart the forgotten truth,
Whisper, whisper through your tongue the words of love,
Whisper, whisper through your nose the scent of your forgotten truth.

Whisper, say it that's all I desire those truthful words,
Whisper, those words of sensuous melodies,
Whisper, for pain no more as you whisper those words of love,
Whisper, whisper not a Chinese whisper, but a word of pure English,
                    a word we both shall understand

Whisper, whisper. Hush! Hush! Don't cry! Just whisper a little,
Whisper, whisper be not a chocolate bar but a rose of pure passion,
Whisper, whisper these lyrical looney tunes thus near an end,

Whisper, whisper we're so in love, so make love to me like a bird
                    of paradise
Whisper, whisper, not an eagle or a parrot, not even a cockateil
                    can compare to you,
Whisper, whisper, change the record love, just be my true love
                    until the day we die
Whisper, whisper this day is near, but as long as I'm with you
          for not does it matter as out love will shine and
                    death will be just a change of scenery

Whisper, whisper, it's time to go to sleep, think not of a mermaid's
                    breast, just an angel's Heaven.
Whisper, whisper, sound asleep I can hear your sweet harmless
                    breathing into my ear,
Whisper, whisper, wipe those tears for no fears. No longer you're
          the burning embers in the night-time glimmer like a
                    fluttering candle.
Whisper, whisper in the summer the butterflies glide gently by and
                    in the winter the snowmen smile at the sun,
But as long as I'm with you I need never whisper, so in love I am.

Gaz Thompson

TULIPS IN THE DARK

By the light of my front window
I see them standing in the night air.
Their scentless dignity
defies me to pick them.

Usually unseen in the darkness
I am surprised to find them there
in their private world
still keeping their own secrets.
They are as boldly red and yellow
as daylight flowers.

Do hidden words
like them
remain as bright?

Deirdre Armes Smith

I PROMISED

When I read B N Louis' lines
'I will love you until
the moon replaces the sun'
I knew my promise had to be broken
No words I wanted to write this day
For the poet in me is always at work.
Now I know why there will be no other love
For poets are forever pampering me.
Folks are always witnessing my smile
For 'Kerry' poetic beauty is always echoing around.
I love you poets, what more can I say
Your words make me feel more than divine.

Carolie Pemberton

WITHIN DARKNESS

Darkness. Rounded. No hard corners.
Obscure shadows. Vague patterns.
Purple blurs - shades of grey.

Clandestine:
A hiding place for lovers
Moments of tender expression.

Interposed by wavering light and
The loneliness of fear.
A favourite time to expire!

Wrestling with new life.
Feeding crying babes:
Neonate - welcome to the world.

Shadowy verdant promenades
In sleepy dells
Shadows dusky trees tangled indigo.

Slowly, a reluctant moon
Casts her glow and sets
The cosmos blazing.

Windows touched by light reveal lovers
Luminous interludes define sleeping babes
Radiance transcends, magical.

Nature changes formation
Alters the rhythm of the night
God laughs: We bow. Tremble before an icon.

The silver lady emboldens the tide
Paints molten curves on the restless waves
Encircles the earth with her own constellation.

June Crosby Jackson

REMIND ME AGAIN

Small, slow, skipping gait,
Slightly comical to view,
Arthritic limbs struggle to balance,
Tightrope walking easier to do.

'How do I make a cup of tea?
Remind me again.'

Cobwebs settle on grey ridges,
Smoothing each synapse,
Smothering flames,
Thoughts lapse.

'How do I get in?
Remind me again.'

Where love, laughter,
Creativity used to abound,
Vast empty spaces,
Fear of the world around.

'How do I switch the radio on?
Remind me again.'

Sadness for loss
Frustration and rage,
Body still there
Watching essence fade.

'Who are you my dear?
Remind me again.'

She would hate it,
If she was aware.
Alas, she's too busy,
Seeking the bits still there.

'Who am I my dear?
Remind me again.'

Is it hereditary?
Will genes win?
There goes me
Twenty years in.

Sheila Wicks

REFLECTIONS

The top tavern is a dancing room,
where men still drink and drool;
but not to rinse their heaving chests,
as they used to.

The supermarket stands on the main mill,
and monolithic shells,
with silent bells,
cast dull reflections of the times.

There is no reflection on cold grey grills
that stifle a curious eye;
no reflection of mee-maw girls;
no need to shout over rattling looms
or clog cobble compositions
of flat-capped beaus.

No grimy grins stare back
from fiery frames, built to last,
burnt out now,
like explosives tamped too soon to see
the accusing fingers fall
and Hades hoist wheels stilled.

Tom Hill

THE WINTER ACONITE

Gold cup shining from hoar-covered grass
Encircling ruffled collar of green
You come each winter as in years past
To bring to our world your tender gleam.

Dear sweet harbinger of spring
Braving the elements of cold and wind
In frost and snow, beauty you bring
Your burnished gold lying undimmed.

'Your life gives a message, what do you say?
Gold can be found on the darkest day.'

Margaret Renshaw

DEATH IN SPRING

The countryside looks lovely now
as blossom bursts on cherry bough
The rolling fields are green and lush
the skylark sings and merry thrush
Golden beds to daffodils
carpet woodland fells and hills
New lambs clamber to their feet
and finding voices start to bleat
The cattle graze quite unaware
that death is all around them there.

Soon the slaughter will begin
the white clad men demeanour grim
Prepare their weapons for the task
hooded heads and faces masked
The cattle sensing start to run
but have no chance to beat the gun
Bodies piled up everywhere
the stench of burning fills the air
Farmers stare in disbelief
at empty fields once filled with sheep.

Margaret Martin

THE FAVOURITE

A father's favour divides a family
as clean-cut as the wind
divides the corn

brothers lie idle in festering fields
skinned raw by famine
and abrasive memories

their father paid a seven-year price
for a son, Rachel-born
Joseph, the dreamer
favoured by a covetable coat

they dipped it in borrowed blood
a substitute death
to lacerate a father's heart
and sold the dreamer south
along a route planned by others

but the journey was his own

dragged from pit to prison
where dreams became him
he rose to a virtual throne

after a seven-year harvest
he fed his hungry brothers.

Angela Butler

FELLTOP COMMUNION

The Muse and I Communion take
upon the haughty fells,
In tranquil isolation
where I, a mortal speck
humbled fall before
My Soul's Elixir -
her vast . . . airy
Other World
Dimension
and the Earth at my feet
cleansed with her rains,
the tears of her
Holy Waters
wringing out the hurt and
contamination of callous
civilisation,
humanity a blemish on her
beauty,
a weakness in her
wilderness
seeking to destroy that
Other Worldliness in
Time
Invoking

Unworthy of her
Blessing . . .

Carolyn Smith

CORRA LINN
(For my mother)

Though artists, and poets, found you worthy of praise,
By the pull of the lade; and the turn of the wheel,
They would harness your power and your dignity steal.
And out children spilled, like ants from their hill,
For they too would live to serve Owen's Mill.
And if your strength was stolen; in truth so was theirs,
As each day they poured down the wells of the stairs.
But, then, they could dance; could skip and could play,
As the dreams of their childhood slipped slowly away . . .
And down you still tumble, beyond the racemill,
As we pause here awhile on the brow of the hill.
And our thoughts stray to how, they too, must have been,
Inspired by the story of all that we've seen . . .

Robert Carson

HUNTER'S MOON

Misty veil surrounds the moon,
Suspends her in a soft cocoon;
Her ghostly opalescence bathes
Hushed, slumbering land in gentle swathes.
O'er contours of dark vales and hills
Moist, dewy mantle floats, and chills
The heart of every wooded hollow,
Yet, still, the stealthy fox must follow
Tracks and scents to satisfy
Deep hunger; yes, the end is nigh
For unsuspecting prey ahead,
Tonight his family will be fed.
Sleek, russet form through shadow slips
And disappears where hedgerow dips.

In haunting flight the owl sweeps by;
How silent motion can belie
A strength of talon, poised to strike,
On sensing mouse by yonder dyke.
The silence of the hour dictates
This nightly hunter stares . . . and waits.
In swaying solitude he bides,
For Mother Nature will provide.
Bright, rippling stream now eerie seems,
Awash with moonlight's silvery beams;
Her whispering, sighing way she wends,
Meandering on to journey's end
As night steals by at Heaven's command,
And moonlight now takes dawn's fair hand.

Kay Spurr

VISITING THE HOME

I arrive to find you drifting
Going to (or from?) your room
Looking cross and agitated
Your world so full of gloom

You see me and look delighted
Sudden pleasure in your eyes
So I smile and say 'Hi Mum!'
Thinking you recognise

But the moment is just fleeting
Soon you're asking me my name
Your memory's been defeated
I wonder why I came

You've forgotten I'm your daughter
And don't remember my dad
A whole lifetime deleted
Things we did -fun we had

For you live in your own world now
And there's nothing I can do
I miss you mum - and wish you
Could know how I love you

Chris Waddington

FAITH ALWAYS RESPONDS

To say that 'We believe in God' means what?
That God manipulates our puppet springs?
This world's some clockwork toy, its once tight springs
Unwinding towards a void where God is not?
Or is this earth a playpen, set aside
While God completes His cosmic work elsewhere,
Meanwhile we dwell content but, unaware,
Have lived and worked and blithely multiplied?
Not so! The Christian *'We'*, two thousand years
Has held that God is Love, provides for man,
Has entered hist'ry, sacrificed His son,
Has offered Grace, has wept because He cares!

An academic faith does not make sense.
Belief in God necessitates response.

John Beazley

THOUGH I WALK THROUGH THE VALLEY OF DEATH

Yeah though I walk through the valley of the shadow of death
I shall fear no evil
For thou art my tarnished Nemesis
The one who p****d on my soul

You took my hand and offered me the strength of your protection.
Then I supported you through the darkness of night and the
shadows of dawn. I held you up when I was tired and carried your
load with my own.

Yeah though I walk over littered shards of broken glass,
I shall fear no feeling of pain
For thou art my fallen angel
The one who chewed out my heart?

You wiped away my salted tears, and promised I'd never know sorrow.
Then I rocked your body as you sobbed until dry, and stroked the sweat
from your dampened hair I drowned in your heartbreak, I cared.

Yeah though I waltz with the demons of Hell
I shall fear no taint on my spirit
For thou art my evil oppressor
The one who gouged out my eye.

You told me you'd love me as I yearned to be loved. Then I gave
you my all for forever. I fought with your fears and drove them away.
I bore all your need and I loved.

Yeah though I walk through the streets of depression, through
the alleys of desperation and along the paths of loneliness. Though
I traipse up the hills of despair on the pavements of pain and down
the hills of regret.

I shall fear nothing.

For although you are gone

I am stronger.

Susan Simpson

DAWN BREAKS

The dawn breaks bringing changes to a
sky as black as ink.
A mottled hue develops of blueish
purple pink
The stillness of the night is fading
with the dawn
Sparkling diamond dew drops glisten on the lawn.
The birds begin their morning serenade
as the dark mantle of night slowly begins to fade.
There's a glow in the sky where
the sun will rise
while the owl to his resting place flies
the early riser stirs in his bed and awakes.
As night turns to day
and the dawn breaks.

Joan Chadwick

THE KISS

You kissed my mouth!
And your face
Was smooth and wet
The skin quite cold.

I felt the rain
Swirling round my feet
Rivulets sliding from
My hair, down my back.

Your body was warm
Close against mine,
My fingers in your hair
And the heat of your response.

I could hear the gulls
Screaming overhead,
And the crash of the sea
In the wind and rain

As I touched your face
I wanted to hold this moment!
To explore your features
And remember, for all time.

The softly falling rain
Your kiss!
And the sweetness
Of your love.

That rainy day in September!

Joan Wills

CALTHWAITE VILLAGE SEAT

I love to sit on the village seat
With little birds around my feet.
Beneath the trees standing tall
Lies the path to Calthwaite Hall.

How stately stands Calthwaite Hall,
Its residents known to one and all,
This family that was the mainstay
Of the village life of yesterday.

How soon the time will pass us by
When to the family we'll say 'Goodbye'.
'Good luck, good health to you,' we'll say,
'We'll think of you when you're away.'

Across the road near at hand
Lives a man called Jim Plowman;
A man who works hard in the wood
And for the village does so much good.

'Thank you Jim Plowman,' we all say
'For all your help in every way.
We know and see the work you do.
There would be no sports without you.'

Along the road the Globe Inn stands.
Many times it has changed hands,
But I fear the time is very near
This quaint old pub might disappear.

By the Globe the smithy stood;
In this place it looked so good.
The horses there in all their gear
Waiting to be shod by Eric Reay.

Across the road was the joiner's shop;
This lovely village had the lot!
Here were the pumps with petrol for sale
Served by the owner, Jack Grisdale.

Oh how the village now has grown;
Everywhere they're building new homes,
But there's still the church where we meet
I love to sit on the village seat.

Francis Allen

OUTSIDE LITTLE MORETON HALL (CHESHIRE)

Existing since the fifteenth century,
Enlarged over later years.
How many generations of footsteps
Have echoed along pathways?
Gazed at the great exterior timbers
Set out in diverse patterns?
You pass through the ancient south wing gatehouse
Of this moated manor house,
Cobbled courtyard has many tales to tell.
Interweaving vines, trefoils,
Ancient motifs and friezes greet your gaze.
Near the north west corner porch
Strange quatre-foils are carved from solid wood,
Representing days gone by.
Gabled bay windows spy on visitors.
Black and white timber framed house,
Surviving years, brings pleasure here and now.
Tell us all your dark secrets.

Angela Pritchard

EASTER TIDINGS

On Good Friday, the earliest bluebells began peeping
Between the tufts of wood rush and droves of wild daffodils;
A gaiety of blooms 'neath the coppice fringing the Duddon's flow. . .
Today it is a different music;
White narcissi gently nod above the Melbreak vale,
And a lovely old English thrush flutes his verses
To float away in the pale air -
Across the river's brimming, eddying flow
Past the great oaks and clustered farmsteads to the hills away . . .
Without price too is to walk the hilly cobbles
Of the ancient drover's way by Rogerscale,
Fringed with its cherry trees and fairest primroses . . .
And once again behold the tiny flowers of mosehatel
Studding the bank; fairy blooms of Eastertide,
Making a mystery and at peace with all creation.

John Sears

WAR

The young boy's feet are bare,
The pain on his face beyond compare.
No home, no friends, no bed,
His family all dead.

The silence of the stricken streets,
Is broken when the siren beats
Its loud and nauseating sound
That tells us all that war is bound.

The boy no longer can withstand
The brutal horrors of this kind.
He falls, his head within his hands.
Not far away a soldier stands.

And still the siren goes on sounding,
The fighter's engines go on pounding.
The deadly noise grows loud and dense,
The inane scream breaks his sense.

His future now is just a blur,
This is too much for him to bear.
Tears start to blind him, he's out of control,
He opens his mouth, he's trying to call . . .

For the help he needs that is not there.
The world is lost and no-one cares.
Groaning with death the buildings fall,
Each brick lets out its mercy call.

In the air, engines run,
Do they realise what they've done?
A noise, a flash, a plane is shot,
Smoke starts to billow, the air is hot.

Young pilot's voices start to rise,
Flames compete to engulf the skies.
Just one more death to increase the score,
How many more await death's door?

Should man's folly reek such devastation?
The breaking up of Arab Nations.
Could world peace be brought much nearer?
Is the price they're paying, so much dearer?

Starting war and forming foes,
Has opened up so many doors.
The peace now found might not have been,
And Allied forces never seen,
If these greedy men had not wanted more
And started up this pointless war.

Kathryn J Wilkin

THE SPIRITED ONE

Who dared upset the spirited one
To crush it with one deadly blow.
Did nobody look at the history books
Did nobody advise about protocol
Although her heart ached
For quite a while
She just went on with
That wonderful smile.

Don't think you spirited one
That your life is ended,
Just keep to what you believe
If you slip the traces for a while.
Don't change your lovely ways
Although your heart aches awhile
Just you come back
With that wonderful smile.

Your life's before you spirited one
Be kind, considerate and listen.
You learn such a lot from this
You'll settle down but it takes time
Must love and have kind things to say
Helping people on their way.
As you travel here and there along life's highway
With that wonderful smile.

Gina J E H

YOU'RE NOT ALONE . . .

For those who exist who feel pain,
Whatever the reason, feel pain.
Of the body, of the mind,
It twists you inside,
And you know you'll never
Be the same again . . .

For those who exist, who feel pain,
Whatever the reason, feel pain.
Of the soul, of the heart,
It tears you apart,
And you know you'll never
Be the same again . . .

I hold out my hand to you,
I want you to know that
There's someone who cares
And I want you to know that
You're not alone,
You're not alone.

Jaki Florek

JUBILEE

A love of British Heritage
In England reigns supreme,
Our loyalty we freely give
To a beloved Queen,
Thro' years of strife, undaunted
Our unity has grown,
With an undivided homage
To a stately English throne.

Elizabeth, Her Majesty
Proud sovereign is she,
To wish her joy and happiness
Sing for her Jubilee.

From peaceful English countryside
To rolling hill or down,
When bells will sound to honour her
Ringing with fond renown,
Come join with us to celebrate
Her Golden Jubilee,
God Bless our Queen and country
Forever fair and free.

N Porter

TODAY AND TOMORROW?

The world today is quite different
To that when I was young.
We had little money on which to live
And always lived within our means,
Spending only what we could afford.
Today things are quite different,
Thoughts are that before marriage,
A house, car, furniture and oft-times a child
Are pre-requisites for the future life!
A plastic card is the key
And money, it seems, is presumed to be there
Rather than existing, unarguably, in a bank account.
Xmas and children's birthdays
Are occasions for excessive spending
On toys to match, or out-do
Those received by their schoolfriends -
Bills to be thought about later.
Mr Micawber would have been horrified!
As indeed are we older folk,
Still blessed with an orderly sense of values
Which seem totally lacking today.
There is a sad decline in overall standards,
Which include speech and general manners,
Plus excessive worship at the altar of hedonism -
These bode ill for the future.
It happened to the Roman empire
In years long past!
Will it happen to Britain
In the not-too-distant future?

W S Goodwin

CYBER CHAT

Topics of conversation; there are many.
Hundreds; some not worth a penny.
Everyone has their own point of view.

Flipside chat; offers you!
Look; see and maybe take up a thread.
Interact; on what someone else said.
Personal issues; you want to share?
Signed up; then get it up there!
Inside these World Wide Web pages.
Digital expression; is in the early stages.
Ever wondered where it could lead?

Annette Smith

AN INTERESTING PROPERTY

An interesting property for the discerning buyer
With tremendous possibilities. (The price should be much higher)
The district is most desirable. The views are quite unique.
Some of the building's original features border on antique.
The roof needs some attention but the rafters are quite sound
And several of the missing slates are still lying on the ground.
The building has potential for extensive renovation.
It is also on a direct route to the railway station.
The garden, though slightly overgrown, conceals exotic blooms
Whilst the house itself contains no less than 7 fair-sized rooms.
The kitchen would respond quite well to a general overhaul.
The lounge could be extended by removing the dining room wall.
Bedrooms 1 and 2 would converge as would bedrooms 3 and 4.
It should be a simple matter to re-hang the bathroom door.
A natural open aspect is enjoyed at the building's rear
The undergrowth is not too dense to spot occasional deer.
A grant is a strong incentive to modernise the plumbing
But do not hesitate too long, more viewers will be coming.
This kind of opportunity does not occur every day.
Cash would be advantageous. A mortgage could cause some delay.

Christina Anglesea

DRACULA

O Dracula, you are so scary
Your nails are claws, your hands are hairy,
The dripping blood on your pointed teeth
Is preventing me from going to sleep.

O Dracula, you are so mean,
Your eyes keep turning red from green,
Your bat-winged cloak is like the night
I'm reluctant to turn out the light.

O Dracula you are so frightening
Your laugh is just like thunder and lightning
Your raucous wolf packs are so mad
I'm going to have to call my dad.

My dad says vampires are not real
So he and I have done a deal,
If I go to sleep straight away
I can go out tomorrow for the day.

Dad has some boxes in the basement
Which his Transylvanian mate sent
We're going to take them all to Whitby
Then on a boat trip to the Black Sea.

Christine Karalius

A PRIVATE THOUGHT IN GROWING UP

The mind is young
The flesh is weak
The heart is tender too
You make me cry
You make me weep
You make me so I cannot sleep
Yes! It's just another bloody day -
But someone's got to pave the way
And if we all got tired
And away we went.
Our lives, I'm sure would be quickly spent
But what the hell - it's just another bloody day.
I've got a broken heart myself
So I can understand the pain.
It never seems the sun will shine
You're forever in the rain
Faces come and go away
And you never ask them
Do they wanna stay?
There's more to life and feelings too
So spare a thought
For the ones that love you.
It may not be the love you want
For there are a hundred ways to love
In many shapes and forms - for you see
The sun sets high for us all
So if you ever need a pal
You know just where to call.
So what the hell - it's just another
Bloody day . . . but keep that chin up
When you go away.

Dee Collins Rowe

THE TUNNEL

I can't seem to think,
I don't know what to do,
My life has turned dark
But the skies remain blue.
I'm stuck in a tunnel
And I can't see the light,
It's a struggle through the day
And I can't sleep at night,
I'm scared I won't make it.
there's a long way to go,
I wish I could say that I will
But I really don't know
I'll just have to wait
And hope for the best
And try and get rid
Of this weight on my chest.
Because it's holding me back
And I want to proceed,
But I don't know if it's worth it
Or if I'll even succeed.
As you've probably realised
I've lost all self esteem,
And it's finally hit me
That this life isn't a dream
But I have got over
The shock and the fright,
But I've been left in this tunnel
And I can't see the light.

Mark Allen

THAT FRIDAY FEELING

I've got that Friday feeling
And it has started in my belly
My good vibes now touch the ceiling
It's far better than watching telly

We're going out this Friday night
Gonna get absolutely wasted
The vibes are good, the time is right
For the best booze you've ever tasted

Give me a coke, give me a beer
Whatever the drink is fine
Just make sure that the loos are near
I'm sure we'll have a great time

Marie Levine

NIGHT-TIME

In the stillness of the night,
The sea whispers softly as it laps under the sand.
No gentle breeze disturbs the trees
No moon does rise above the clouds
Even the traffic is silent
No birdsong, no sirens
Just the stillness of the night.

The patter of raindrops upon my window pane,
Suddenly a soft breeze disturbs the trees
As the first rays of dawn break through the clouds
And sleeping seabirds awaken to
Disturb the stillness of the night.

Pale sunlight filters through the trees
And dawn gives way to day
Little children come out to play
The stillness of night has gone astray.

S Peach

MOVING ON

We feel betrayed, lost and undone
Our partner has left
With another they have run,
Do not be unhappy, do not feel sad
After the initial shock
You can start your new life
A whole new world awaits, be glad
Nobody's slave you can do what you like
Look after number one
The rest can take a hike,
Get yourself sorted
Lots of things you can do
The world is your oyster
Do whatever suits you
Move on, be positive
You will feel better by far
From now on forever
You are the star

Terry Butler

REFLECTION

If I can stay sleeping
Through tide's turn,
Waves lapping round my feet,
Stay sleeping, never waking,
Till water
Waist-high oozes
And invades my space,
And still sleep on,
Awakening to awareness
When lungs cease only,
Then, have I won?
Who knows?
I cannot hold the tide
And he who tries
Finds no repose.

Moira Taylor

FLICKERING FLAMES

The sky is bright.
Day or night.
Licking flames, burn and glow
Smouldering smoke goes high and low.
The fire rages fast and slow.

The firemen rush as fast as they can go,
But still flames flicker, high and low.

The air is hot
The crowds gather at the spot
The fire dies with water and wind
The smoke smoulders on and on.

Euan George James Tiernan (11)

THE OBSERVER

A mysterious man on this cold, clear night
Stands stirred by stars in the clearness alight,
Alone this frosty hour
His eyes search and scour
He sees a mystical power
In the part of the cosmos revealed to sight

Pondering the birth of each distant star,
And contemplating the light-years . . . how far?
What came to make and to mould
The heavens so vast and old,
The constellations in the cold
Remind how minute we of this world are.

Creations of mankind shall seem so small
When remote galaxies seem to flare and fall,
Thought cannot comprehend
A beginning or end,
A comet's path shall wend
Into infinity - then fade beyond recall.

Science, which over God claims victory
Knows not the star's source - nor their history.
Though science has resolved
All enigmas shall be solved
Why and how the stars evolved,
Is this not the eternal mystery?

Anthony Quinn

UNTITLED

I reflect
In retrospect
And contemplate
The past

Its achievements
Its happiness
Its memory
Its sorrow

And I embrace
The future
And the scope
Of its potential

Mark Thomas

RACING THE UNHEARD

Over sand swept by time and tide
The endless wait drifts slowly by.
Tossed and turned on bed of rock,
Fought battles killed, beaten and lost.
Frayed endings caught as fly in web,
Sprayed victory of a curious dead.

So cliched even when man fades,
Effervescent are his tidal waves.

Now water foams with memory,
The eternity we never knew deplete.
Ever long this war will rage,
'Tween beauty and mankind's ran race
To be supreme, to rule the world,
Forgetting oceans never heard.

Helen Marshall

HAPPENINGS

Whatever happened to you and me
We threw it all away, didn't we?
Drifted apart, like rolling waves.
We had it all, and let go.

We could have made it so good and right,
But love sneaked away, somehow.
I sometimes think, life's a heavy heart
In fact, I'm now quite sure.

Yeah, we had it all, and let go so stupidly.
I wanted to say more, but my head said 'No!'
Maybe it was because we were too young.
Yes, I think so!

Heavy hearts, die young, mine did so
From that time, long ago.

Terry Ramanouski

LIFE

At seventy you begin to see life's pattern.
What to you in life, has really happened.
We are like the vessels which the potters form
God is working on us, from the time we are born.

Growing, changing, learning day by day
God gives us blessings along our way.
Many stages, we have to go through
So we don't thwart, God's plan for me and you.

In many ways we are certain to struggle,
In life's long process, we learn to juggle.
At all times and in every situation.
God won't push you past your limitation.

Broken and wounded we try to give up,
You say I can't go another day, in this rut
You're still in God's hands, He's always with you,
He knows every hair on your head, He will see you through.

Suddenly you understand, you have three score and ten
That your life will soon be coming to an end.
Each extra day, you thank our Lord above
Try your best to give out more of His love.

Sylvia M Harbert

NEW FRIEND

Over the years since you left me alone,
I've cried so many tears.
Part of my heart went with you,
The rest was filled with fears.
How will I cope?
What will I do?
Who do I talk to and how?

These were a few of my concerns,
But I don't have them now.
I found a friend to talk to,
Someone who really cares.
Someone who shows compassion,
Though never utters a word.

He's led me through the darkness,
Till once again I could see the light.
Held my hand when I felt weak and brought me
comfort during the night.
The person I lost was my dear mum,
Whom I loved with all my heart.
That friend I found was God up above,
Who helped me make a brand new start.

Dorothy Davies

THE WALK

The most perfect day would have to be
A walk in the country, just you and me
Over rolling hills and fields of green
We stop for a moment and sit by the stream
To gaze at wild flowers with colours so bright
Which dazzle the day and light up the night
Then winding our way down an old country road
Pass crumbling walls and buildings of old
Which once stood strong, sturdy, alive
Now just a ruin, I look and I sigh
We continue our stroll past hedgerows and brambles
Enjoying each moment of this peaceful ramble
We hear the birds singing their beautiful song
The warm wind whispers as we walk along
The hours have passed but time means nothing
When I am with you, sharing and loving
As the day draws in and the light starts to fade
The best decision that we have made
A walk in the country it has to be
The perfect day for you and me

Alison Robinson

ADARNA'S SONG

Sing to me Adarna's song
From the mist grey slopes of Mourne
Sing to me Adarna's song
As night flees westward
Over hills so worn -
By wind and rain
Snow and sleet;
By the summer's oven
Autumns rainbow boughs
And paths once worn deep
By the passing of soft elven feet.

Now sing to me of soft sad sighs
And sing to me of children's eyes,
Of laughing smiles and teardrop ears -
Of the dawns and dusks
Of many years:
Years to grow
To reap and sow,
To hear bards sing
Of right and wrong -
While time itself
Shall sweetly be, Adarna's song.

Paul B Whittaker

50P

Has anyone seen 50p?
I put it on the shelf.
I was gonna spend it
On some sweeties for myself.
Obviously, I can't no more
It's gone and ran away.
Oh well, I'll have to save more up
Until another day.
I know that I did put it there
I saw it with my eyes.
Someone must have stolen it
And someone's telling lies.
Whoever's got it - give it back,
Cos it's not fair on me,
Hurry up, the shops'll shut:
I want my 50p!

Tambi Maple

AUTUMNAL THOUGHTS

An autumn leaf spirals its way to the ground
Has fulfilled its life's purpose and now fades without sound
In its full flush of beauty was a joy to behold
Its emerald green colour with the light did unfold
The shape and the texture had the mark of perfection
A true work of Art and was God's own selection.

Other leaves they did follow as their turns they did come
Wafting down from the trees they formed a crisp golden dome
It was heaven to stroll through a forest of trees
And feel that carpet of nature rustling under my feet
The sounds were so soothing they sure calmed the heart
They're a gift of creation, a real integral part.

Those tree shades in autumn are a dazzling display
Their oft changing colours make you just want to pray
From dark green to olive, deep brown to rich gold
The soft tints of pink they ooze beauty untold
Little things mean a lot, is a well-worn expression
Thank God for nature and its simple perfection.

When people ease gently into autumnal years
They store many memories of laughter and tears
The ear of a friend who listens with care
Is much valued and treasured as secrets laid bare
Those declining times can be lonesome and weary
Like the trees stripped of leaves which look oh so 'teary'.

As I rest in our garden on a crisp autumn day
I gaze at the trees lift each branch as if in prayer
The birds feel secure as they nest high above
They warble sweet music which I truly love
My eyes they soak in all the colours around
This is truly my season, a paradise found.

Francis Casey

BEATLE STREET

A view over the bridge
To the other side,
Cast in metal stars
On musical seats -
The yellow brick road
Following the 'Apple'
Lit to perfection in green neon.
Gypsy Romeo's in the Revolution.
Pictures of underworld heroes
Bottled in alizarin and cream.
Ships sailing in the night
Twinn'd to New York and Shanghai.
Letting it be just a clip
From the 'Life' film,
Chips off the old block,
Blue plaqued in Menlove Avenue;
Rocking on
Even in his grave.
The one and only
Played out in the Blue Angel
Flying high by the Epstein statue.
Boarding another plane
To a destination
Where only few may go.
Cool, then collected,
Spiritual warriors
Showing us another world
Where we all could be.

Peter Corbett

A BABY BOY

Today was born a little lad
Bringing joy to his mum and dad
They thought of many different names
But finally settled on Martin James.

Hair of gold, eyes of blue
A beautiful gift from God to you
Ten little fingers, ten little toes
A cute little button for a nose.

What a wonderful gift, a baby boy
Bringing with him such pride and joy
What happy pictures for you to behold
To store in memory as years unfold.

So treasure these years they will soon be gone
For babies grow and time moves on.
From baby to boy from boy to man
And he will be part of God's great plan
With the blessings of being in the family of man.

A Maddock

LANCASHIRE'S LOST HERITAGE

Old Pendle hill, old Pendle, you stand there alone,
fashioned by God, and the wind, rain and snow.
With small villages nestling at thy feet.
Through fields and woodlands by forests and streams
to quaint little mill towns, mills run by steam.
With tersest homes with flagged roofs and flagged streets,
streets paved with stone setts.
You can hear weavers coming and going all day
to the weaving sheds all wearing clogs, clip-clop there they go.
Look at the council workmen repairing the streets,
flaggers and pavers and the tar boilermen.
Look at the binmen with bins, shoulders full of ashes,
from the coal fires that seem to burn day and night.
Milkmen and rag bone men with the old horse and carts.
And what is that smell? Beer brewing at the local breweries.
Butchers and bakers and candle makers,
tradesmen of every trade you could think of in the old mill towns.
But time passes fast, it soon drifts away, and what have we got
                                              left today?
Mills all closed down, tarmac streets and footpaths
our Lancashire heritage seems very easy to forget.
We've to become multi-racial and embrace other faiths and traditions
from all around the world,
and forget our heritage. Why the hell should we
just because the powers that be, say so.

Donald Jay

KIDS

My niece, who is three
Has a vivid imagination.
Her vocabulary is limited,
Though two of her favourite words are;
'No' and 'mine'.

Toys strewn over the living room floor
Are a magnet for your feet.
They always seem to be there as you sneak home late.
Your howls of pain are heard all over the house.

Kids! Don't you just love them?
Though I couldn't eat a whole one.
Christmas time is the worst,
Hide the telly, the mail order catalogues,
Or your bank account will empty so rapidly that
You will still be paying the following May,
I know it's obvious; but what a price to pay.

Be aware that the scenarios that you can find yourself in,
Can lead to more than a sulky din.
Kids are not always that bad,
Just remember that at three years old,
There is no reasoning.

Use your imagination, go to their level,
Teach them a few new words.
Don't get too pally though,
Because come New Year's Eve, guess who
Will be asked to do a 'spot of baby-sitting'?
And as the country jollies,
You will be making jellies.
I don't want to be the one to say 'I told you so!'

Robert Goodier

MANCHESTER

Manchester once an industrial town
Where hatworks and cotton mills did duly abound
Kids worked half-time and were let out of school
And woe betide any truant or playing the fool
The taskmaster's job was so strict and so stern
You had to toil for the money you earn
Bare-footed urchins straight off the street
Employed as bobbin carriers in their bare feet
Time is now the neon glow of the city
Where all the girls look so prim and so pretty
While Grandma and Grandad like to reminisce
It's so long ago since they had their first kiss
Unions now fight for the workers' cause
Just pay your dues and obey all their laws
Roads that once held those gala parades
Are now pedestrian precinct arcades
Mancunians now call the Metropolis a city
By encroaching on other districts, more's the pity.

Francis Arthur Rawlinson

A SENSE OF PLACE

She had been suffering from stress,
The pills didn't seem to work,
From being so active and vital,
Responsibilities she would shirk.
The doctor suggested a holiday,
The change would do her good,
If nothing else would do the trick,
The fresh air, certainly would.
She arrived at a country cottage,
Little windows and strong oak beams,
Just the place to rest a weary head,
But not everything is what it seems.
The rattling started right away,
The groaning much later on,
She realised that all signs of peace,
Had well and truly gone.
She moved to a house not far away,
This one was sunny and bright,
She unpacked her clothes, and bits of things,
And prepared to spend the night.
All her stress seemed to fade away,
She felt warm and quite secure
A couple of weeks residing here,
And she knew she'd find a cure.
There was something magical about this place,
The beautiful garden, the flowers,
She instinctively knew that this was the spot,
To spend some happy hours.
The holiday was nearly over,
But she'd discovered for what it was worth,
You are nearer to God in a garden
Than anywhere else on Earth!

Edith Antrobus

AFTERMATH

The tide departs, unburdened,
relieved of excess baggage.
Driftwood sprawls, stranded,
grotesquely exposed,
embraced by silt and mud.
Bottles skulk warily,
implanted in the sand,
unmasked by gleaming sunlight.

The wind growls, puckish,
cursing scavenging gulls.
Ozone permeates freely,
titillating flaring nostrils,
circling the shore.
An old shoe cowers ruefully,
desolate, hanging by a thread,
afraid of what may come.

The beach reclines, phlegmatic,
lacerated yet unbowed.
Solar rays glimmering gently,
across its open wounds.
Nearby a boat lies vacant,
marooned in ooze and sludge.
The tilt of its posture,
a symbolic cry for help.

Paul Kelly

To Define My Age

I am a man, I exist to defend tenderness,
My own as much as anyone else's.
I face the total chaos of wildest waves
At the core of the physical universe, I play its dice game
In the quest of joining God in creating ordered patterns,
But I recoil from the man who harshly imposes pattern,
From such I run apart wholly wild and free,
Almost into the arms of the lasciviously chaotic,
With almost half their loud barbaric yawp,
I also recoil from the conquest of nature,
The tenderness above all others I am here to defend.
What wonder if imposing on her creates violent storms
As her balance of which we are part is rudely shaken.
I invoke her as God's spouse, a very supreme parent
Who comes to us with all her wonders in heaven when her
                                    most physical form
Disintegrates to a seemingly blank nothingness
For me and my partner to find her most exalted beauty hiding
Secretly in the nothingness, this is mine and my woman's shared task.
I tentatively approach such a woman with caution,
Disappointed she is now not a virgin
Though the temerity of being virgins is still within us
Bringing us so closely together
That there will be larger numbers of mature virgins because of us,
More loving massage and less feverish copulation:
And the massage of the youngsters who appeal to us
Will not be frowned on in a clean-minded world
When I listen carefully to her bodily rhythm
Before we create a special jewel of Love.

Tony Dixon

SMILE!

It's said a smile is priceless
The only thing in life that's free,
Bringing joy and happiness
No one can disagree!

It makes a beggar in the street
The luckiest man alive,
A millionaire is poor without one,
A smile you just cannot buy.

It costs nothing to give one,
It means the world to receive,
Cheering up unhappy people
Making those without faith believe.

So give a little something
Cheer up someone by miles,
Nothing is greater
Than receiving a smile!

Chloe Sweeney (14)

THE FALL

Autumn's chill is in the air,
Its hazy presence everywhere.
Days grow short and nights are long,
And birds are sparing with their song.

Trees rejoice and proudly hold
Aloft their leaves of burnished gold.
(The wind awaits, with pent-up sound,
To whisk them, tumbling, to the ground).

The shadows lengthen, sun is low,
As swifts and swallows homeward go.
Ploughs and harvesters are stilled
And barns with new-mown hay are filled.

The ripened fruits are gathered in,
Firm and full and smooth of skin.
All around church bells are rung
And hymns of Harvest Home are sung.

Frank Jensen

LAMPLIGHT

Victorian mansions
Bought and sold
What secrets, will unfold
When buyers renovate
To bring the property up to date?
What of the ghosts
Of that Victorian past
When houses were made to last
When home was home
No mod cons
In the Victorian era.
But cosy warm fires
And lamps aglow
Comfort and security
And 'folks' that were known.
Doors could be left open
Stress - well - unknown
Life wasn't easy
But family values were 'high'
Courtesy and manners
Did I hear someone say?
Yes, this is 'our way'
But Victorians, paved the way.

Margaret Parnell

ALZHEIMER'S GEAR

He's lost it.
Elderly Gent, confused and lost
sits alone, drinks tea by the lake,
ever watchful, ever thinking.
Brain's in gear - but which gear?

Looks at his watch, wipes the cup,
the table, the spoon.
Leaves the cafe lakeside,
Looks at his watch, confused,
'Where's your coach, Sir?'
Looks at his fist-held tickets
tightly gripped, hazes over.
Brain is in gear -
But which gear?

Roger W Chamberlain

CONCENTRIC DESTINIES

Two independent circles, that sometimes join,
Two separate routes, with similar pathways.
Advise.
Criticise.
Beginning before, and continuing now
Onward, through this journey.
Learning useful knowledge.
Remembering past mistakes from other lives,
Hopefully wisely.
Not needing to share indiscriminately,
But existing solely for mutual benefit.
Comfortable company on occasions,
Laughter and sorrow shared.
Ultimately, respect and honour -
Respect for space, feeling and opinion
Honoured by this friendship.

Tree

LAUGHTER

Laugh and the world laughs with you,
That's what the poets say,
Oh, what a gift is laughter,
We need it every day.
There's so much pain and sorrow
In this old world today,
We need the gift of laughter
To chase the gloom away.
Make somebody feel happy
And you'll find you're happy too,
Through laughter comes much happiness
And lasts the whole day through.
So do not write of doom and gloom
And very soon you'll see
If you write verse to make folks laugh
Then happy you will be.

Margaret B Baguley

PHOTOGRAPHS

Grey - the colour of long ago, deceiving.
Yesterday's not that far away.

Tomorrow will soon be behind,
May be colourful, maybe not.
Love, could stay with you forever
If it comes your way at all.

Maybe it will just pass through, if it's true,
You're one of the few.

Fortune - drops on your lap, don't get excited.
Burns like dry hay - no use in the end.
Fame - everyone knows your name,
Shallow, like the unmarked grave.
The sound is hollow.

Keep tight hold of -hope,
Faith is a precious possession,
In the minds of the dying,
These words are a cure.

Their sleep is pure,
A new day awaits them.

Knowledge - lead to things great and small
The best things are, simple.

Alison McGinty

MANGLE HISTORY

Sopping wet washing
Boiled, soiled wash
Needing more squeezing . . .
Hands, arms, felt red raw
Sheets folded neatly
Wooden tongs gripped clothes
Guiding through rollers . . .

Soaking more washing,
Starched collars and cuffs
Then blown high on lines . . .
Used slatted rack too
In that cold wash-house
Or above the 'Rayburn'
As Grandma's before . . .

Today, Mum's mangle
Is painted bright red
Where geraniums trail . . .
All that is left is
Photograph with frame
As washing machines
Claim to squeeze the same.

Lesley J Worrall

FAREWELL CENTURY OF TEARS

Ring out the old century.
Ring the bells with vigour and joy.
Farewell the black years,
century of massacres, folly and tears.

Ring out the century of fears.
Close the unclosed eyes
of wasted, sacrificed youth
in fields clothed in blood.

Ring out the century of cares.
Earth weeps with morning dew
the hunted white man,
black man and Jew.

Welcome a new dawn
when humanity
discards inhumanity.
Worthy to clasp the hand of its God.

Robert Allen

WHERE DAISIES GREW

(A Lament)

Then

Our township was once a green oasis,
Quiet backwater from busy Bolton,
Weary shoppers revived by delightful
Encounters, walking home from the bus stop,
Passed fields where lace tablecloths of daisies
Spread a refreshing feast for our eyes;
Heard birdsong, undefeated by traffic,
Space to breathe, time to spare with folks we knew,
Exchanged warm words, met with friendly faces,
Whose natural neighbourliness brought home
The closeness of a small community,
A treasure we were forced to surrender.

Now

Fields have long gone, daisy chains giving way
To Chain Superstores, springing up like weeds,
Estates of new houses, spoiling the view,
Increased population needing more schools,
Bypasses to reach them, whirring wheels
Not wings, banished are our fine, feathered friends;
Silent, stony stares of new Invaders
Offer no crumbs of comfort to my soul,
No sign of interest but their own small world,
I am the stranger in my own hometown,
Missing the old, familiar landmarks,
All sacrificed in the name of Progress.

Olive Miller

THE SAGA OF BARTON AQUEDUCT

We saved a boat from the Breaker's Yard,
Rubbed her down, and stripped her tar,
Sealed her cracks and applied some paint,
And very soon she was shipshape again,
And fit for crossing the Aqueduct.

So, off we set, with our picnic packed,
Bottles of pop, Smiths crisps (and our macs)
Soaking up the sun as we cruised down the Cut -
Waved at by kids and their mangy-looking mutts!
Under Patricroft Bridge bobbed our Lame Duck,
Her cabin still looking like a garden hut -
But sound enough to tackle the Aqueduct.

It was round about then the propeller jammed -
'Til the outboard spat out an old tin can
And we continued leisurely along the Cut,
Standing on deck with our eyes shut
We dreamt of crossing the Aqueduct.

'Nothing can stop her!' I shouted with glee
As Mike poured us both cups of tea,
But the rain came down like stair rod rails,
Blew the summer breeze into a Force Five Gale
And put paid to us crossing the Aqueduct!

Betty Lightfoot

To Peter

My special place to sit and muse
Whether it be wet or dry
I can admire my garden views
Scan the ever-changing sky

I watch the rain come hurtling down
I'm sat here, snug and warm
And passers-by with brollies crowned
Are rushing through the storm

Then in the early morning light
While the grass is wet with dew
I see the swallows in first flight
In Heaven's palest hue

Up now and eyes still rubbing
I look out at my lawn
And there two blackbirds breakfasting
Upon the juicy worms

When daylight's gone and stars come out
So slowly, one by one
I sit here thinking all about
This lovely corner of my home.

Joan Fletcher

THE ELIXIR OF LIFE

Speed and beat of hourly pay
distorts the human right.
But the heart is lined with rainbow print
and wrapped in silken forest green.

A sun that lifts with gilt-edge strokes,
Curls silver on the lakes.
Ribbon flow of mountain streams
all clear and fresh with life.

Mountains pushed and carved with ice
took time to etch the skies.
Visions stretch with grandeur,
that breeze the skin with static grace.

Release the soul to fill the air,
embrace the rising mist.
Nerves a shimmer in rays of siminel light,
lacing tensions with some soft and dreamy sprite.

Nature has a feminine grip
for wounds to wash and dry.
The state of free emotion,
is the elixir of life.

Maria Bernadette Potter

LOSING WALLONIA

Always, the billowing hills
were last to be found,
and springs fell around
dereliction of mills.

Always, the unrisen breeze
would blend with an avenue,
warping the trees
on an under-viewed land.

Always, the weather would win,
with everything damp
or as untouched as dusk.

Then, every hidden Belgian end
was warping, almost-used.

Will Daunt

THE UNSEEN THREAT

I wander over the green fields
Proud to have them as my own,
Been passed down through generations
Many a good seed has been sown.
Our cattle grazing quietly
Waiting to be milked.
The sheep in yonder meadow
Their fleece as soft as silk.

Then suddenly, a threat appears
Right from out of the blue,
A thing that farmers dread most
And hope it won't happen to you.
Alarm bells ring, our hearts beat fast
This disease is then declared,
And overnight like a nightmare,
I have lost my herd.

My life's work now goes up in flames,
I cannot bear to think.
My eyes are blurred, through tears and smoke,
My heart begins to sink.
How will I pick up from this blow?
I must be brave and bold
And start again when all is clear
Before I get too old.

Flo E Smith

RAINBOW

If I could catch a rainbow,
I would do it just for you,
I'd share with you its beauty
On days when you were feeling blue.

If I could build a mountain
I'd do it just for you
I'd make it a place of sincerity,
A place we could call our own,
A place where we could be alone.

But all of these things,
I'm finding impossible to do,
I can't build a mountain,
Or catch a rainbow just for you.

But there is something I can do for you,
And that something is to love you,
To hold you, to care for you
And to stop you feeling blue.

Sioux McDonnell

RETAIL THERAPY

Outside the rain is pouring down
I cannot venture into town.
Another boring, rainy day,
can't seem to wash these blues away.
Don't want to pop another pill
it only serves to make me ill.
I'll sit down here and make a list
of all those things that can't be missed.
That leather coat I saw last week,
a bargain price and oh so chic.
The shirt I saw would look so fine,
those trousers too if they were mine.
A CD here, a CD there,
the trouble is they're everywhere!

Another day and the sun shines down.
With my glad rags on I hit the town.
I'm feeling better with every mile,
the more I spend, the more I smile.

Another rainy, windy day
and with my finances blown away
I'm feeling really rather blue,
well, what's a poor boy meant to do!
I think I really need that pill
even though it makes me ill.
I'll sit down here and make a list
of all those things that can't be missed
and oh what pleasure there will be
on my next fruitful shopping spree!

John Taylor

THE GIFT OF HOPE

A shooting star flashed across the sky one day
Everything seemed so strange and it lost its way
It had been raining and a rainbow came into view
All its wonderful colours made a reflection hue
The lost star had landed on the top of the rainbow
And it could not move so waited patiently for it to go
Perched there looking around it saw many, many things
Everything seemed bright and clear, wished it had wings
In that moment it seemed to see the whole world of light
So this was a truly magical power, it had been given sight

It saw the wonder of the universe
As fragrant blossom burst into bloom

It saw happiness and prosperity
In the healthy in body and mind in tune

It saw sickness and sadness
Those who are in need of comfort and care

It saw needless violence and tensions
Cultures as they live together, hard to bear

It saw where compromise and tolerance
Can see life's true miracles come to pass

If only it could be accepted by the mass

So maybe if you wish on that shooting star high up above
Each one collected, then held closely to its heart with love
When the rainbow is no more and the star floats back again
To whence it came, yet to return in all its glory to attain
Still bearing that most wondrous-given power to offer
Freely to those who want to believe in its precious proffer
                    The gift of Hope.

Octavia Hornby

THE SEA

Alone I stand searching the sea,
Watching seagulls, mocking overhead,
With blue clouds chasing across the sky;
Seeing the world, so different with new expression.

The rhythm of singing sea, is flowing with smiling glances
May the beauty joys making lullaby wave-line
Bringing the pleasure of life, breeze beauty,
Welcome with summer horizon.

Watching the boats moving over the waves
And far away from the shore,
Flickering in daylight motion
Into some sea, valley journey.

Rocks are sculpted into all shapes and sizes
Surrounded by the sea echoing waves,
Watching the sunrise over the rocks
It has a cool, beautiful salty appetite.

Heather Aspinall

CHAIN OF LINKS

The link in the chain has severed,
For all eternity
And often we ask ourselves
Why did this happen to me?

But we never get an answer
Not that satisfies our sorrow,
All we can do is hope
For a better tomorrow.

Great pain is caused by this passing
A sorrow never to heal
Waking brings such sadness
Can this ache be real?

People say time's a great healer
And deep down we know it's true
But what happens till then . . . you wonder,
How will you get through?

When my chain was broken,
And the sorrow hard to bear
I placed my hands together
And whispered a silent prayer.

I survived the trauma
The pain eased after years
But I wish the link could have been mended,
And put an end to my tears.

Winnie Milnes

ODE TO LYTHAM BEACH

The Seven Seas have been explored and all the lands in each.
There is nowhere in them I declare, as nice as Lytham beach.
The Windmill sails set to the west, the setting sun beseech
that it returns tomorrow to smile down on Lytham beach.

The Lifeboat House Museum tells of times now out of reach,
of tragedy, heroism, played out from Lytham beach.
Churches stand against the wind and face their weathered fate.
Schools that they supported, moved, to bring them up to date.

St Peter's and St John Divine with still a lot to teach
the people on a Sunday as they walk on Lytham beach.
The jetty going down in mud, the boats no longer reach.
it wasn't always like that though, down on Lytham beach.

Once there was a pier, sandpits, swings, donkey rides as well,
a boating pool where little lads, their fantasies could swell.
The Pierrots put on quite a show in their theatre of green,
now each year we have the Proms, fireworks and 'The Queen'.

The little Cottage Hospital and the Clifton Arms Hotel,
one to cure, one to pamper, both to make us well.
Lowther Gardens, theatre, tennis, bowling, all in easy reach,
of the prom and broad green sward that makes up Lytham beach.

As light descends out in the west abaft of Charlie's mast
The shrimp boats ride the rising tide, anchored, home at last.
The evening sun highlights the boats, a cormorant on each.
The sun will shine tomorrow, that's for sure on Lytham beach.

When we've done our roaming, sands of time begin to leach.
I can think of nowhere nicer than to overlook the beach.
To watch the tides race in and out, the moon to wax and wane.
Gaze at Southport, Winter Hill - it's clear! We could be in for rain.
With a glass of wine, a telescope, I'd think that life's a peach,
If I could settle into dotage, on unique Lytham beach.

Derek B Hewertson

IT'S AMAZING

It's amazing what you find
At the bottom of boxes:
Toys from your childhood,
Stuffed birds and foxes.
Old calculators,
Anniversary cards,
Measurements on paper
Written in yards.

It's amazing what you find
At the back of your attic:
Posters from when
You were a boy-band fanatic!
Last winter's woollies,
Children's school books,
Their paintings and pictures
And rusty coat hooks.

It's amazing what you find
When you just take a look.
What you treasure fondly,
To others seems junk.
But you know what they mean,
What memories they hold.
So keep them forever,
No matter how old!

Mila Pandav

FIXTURE

You know nothing of my existence, do you?
And yet the beat of your heart
comforts me while I sleep,
a gentler beat
than the one that shook your diaphragm
on Saturday night and, diffusing through fluid,
bathed me in pulsating sound.

Soaking up the stimuli of
strobe light and colour,
the harsh, staccato tones of voices raised
lifted me from slumber.

At first, I did not like the shocking surges
through my blood
but now, I cannot wait to sense the buzzing in my ears.
It feels so good,
so, soon, I'll smack you with a kick
then you can fix me up.

Oh, this is magical:
a plush, red cathedral
and the heat of radiation causing waves,
optical eddies of convected currents
in my fluid world.
Aniseed and nicotine bathing me
in this reducing atmosphere of dizzy joy.
The source of heat and light is high
but not as high as me and you,
we two are one beneath the blistering sun.

You know nothing, do you
In your dark and silent world?
No more, the nights of ecstasy,
for you have killed his love for me
and our summer in the sun is at an end.

I will take my malice out on you,
you spoiler set in dark and bloody walls.
That cell is soon to give you up.
You do not know your time has come,
sitting, as I am, in a sterile clinic hall.

John Tirebuck

OUR VISIT TO BLACKPOOL

We went to Blackpool for a few days
There we watched the high waves
The sea was very rough
The wind was extremely tough
It was an icy wind that did blow

We stayed in a hotel called Clarron House
It was nice and bright
Everything was done just right
The painting is all white and pink
And is extremely distinct

The owners are Ann and Terry
But you needn't worry
They are helpful and willing
The food is delicious and filling
But it costs more than a shilling

There we met a man named Fred
He forgot which knife should butter his bread
His wife Barbara, how she did laugh
But we did not think he was daft
We thought he was a laugh.

George our waiter he was a Jock
But did he know how to use a wok?
He was there at our beck and call
But George he was not very tall
In fact he was quite small.

Edith Wood

LONELINESS

I'm very lonely as I live on my own
At daytime I'm out so I'm seldom alone
But when evening comes and I'm at home
I'm completely cut off except for the phone.

And that is not much use at all
As telewatchers don't want a call
During their programmes, even my best pal
Will only speak in an interval

There once was a beloved friend
I thought my loneliness would end
The friendship failed, my evenings now are spent
More lonely and sad since he went.

Lisa Wolfe

REASONS

In another dimension -
where, I don't care to mention -
a Great Auk meets a Dodo,
claps his wings, screeches 'Hello!
They say on Earth we're extinct.
Yet here you look . . . plump . . . distinct.
Your beak I see curving low.
Your gait is stately - but slow.
Probably it was your girth
which caused you to disappear from Earth.'

The Dodo looks affronted,
'Sadly, you have been misled.
Where I lived, in Mauritius,
we'd have called you - malicious.
All have heard of the Dodo.
Knowledge of Great Auks? So-so.
You've no cause to sneer - or smile.
Men cleared Great Auks off your isle.
I guess your clan all are dead
because of something *spiteful* you said . . .'

After this exchange, the pair
flap their wings, then strut and glare.
Each decides to take a walk,
with the other not to talk.
Soon the Great Auk finds a crowd
of Great Auks all screeching loud
while that Dodo, looking droll,
stares about him on his stroll.
When will he speak? It depends
on how soon he meets his Dodo friends.

C M Creedon

GOLDEN YEARS
(1948-1998)

I started work in forty-eight,
Serving my time, I thought, would be great,
Served right through to fifty-four,
'A time-served sheet metal worker' who could ask for more?

National Service, my next call,
Royal Engineers, had me a ball,
Egypt, Cyprus, in the Middle East,
A rottweiler police dog, what a beast!

Next two years,
Worked very hard,
Got myself married,
To my sweetheart.

Now had a wife,
And then a son,
The years ahead
Meant lots of fun.

Seventy-two brought to an end,
A period of life when I lost a friend,
My dear wife, forty years of age,
Departed this life to an earthly grave.

In seventy-four picked up the threads,
Married Annette, no regrets,
Gained myself another son,
A new mum too, for number one.

Now I've come to ninety eight,
Time to reflect and contemplate,
Our Silver Wedding is shortly due,
My golden years, have silver too!

Howard Croston

YELLOW

Yellow is a soft colour,
Bouncy, sunny and fun.
Yellow is a colour,
A colour of the sun.

A sunflower petal,
The colour of painted metal,
A reflection of care,
A colour that means share.

You can be yellow when you're happy,
And yellow when you're sad,
Yellow when you're really gold,
And yellow when you're bad.

Kara O'Neill (9)

LIFE IS PEACE

The sky is blue, the sky is grey
It changes its mood day by day.
The sun will shine, the sun will stop
Then dark clouds come out on top.
The winds will blow, the winds will cease
Nature can show us peace.
If only life upon this Earth
Could be controlled, a new rebirth,
To live in peace as we are meant
A life rich in sweet content.
To be of one creed, the human race
Then this Earth would be the place,
For happiness and joy to be found
So transmit the word of peace to all around.

Mike Burke

WEALTH OF WORDS

In tranquility hour after hour
pouring over manuscripts.
Delete, add, edit, proof-read.
Were their efforts worth the pain
tailoring and moulding phrases?

Publication is a far-off dream
through lonely hours they forged ahead
thoughts of Blake and Tennyson
were ribbons in their heads.

Did these great men struggle
with the monumental task
to fulfil that far-off dream
that modern writers face?

Great masterpieces they gave the world
heaped with strength and poise.
Were it that they lived today
in a world of controversy and strife

What offerings would they have shared?
What beauty, wealth, what style
Would they have bestowed?

Burgess J Barrow

GIVE PEACE A CHANCE

I can't make peace between Arab and Jew,
or defuse the bombs of a murderous few,
and when hooligans riot I haven't a clue
of how to stop the things that they do.

But I can find peace in the silence within
with a mind that's still from discord and din,
and there can light my own humble flame,
to shine in the darkness of violence and blame.

And I picture a flame in like-minded hearts
all over the world where we all play our parts,
for darkness can't dwell where'er there is light,
no matter how faint or steadfast and bright.

Each little glimmer in its imperfect way
will *give peace a chance* as the songwriters say,
and brighten our hearts as we look to the day,
when God's loving peace will ever hold sway.

Susan Carr

HAIKU

Over half a life
It takes to climb Life's hill of
Experience; and

Only from the peak
Can eternity be seen,
And remain in sight.

Chris Moores

WINNER

W   orthy of the poem of the year
I   lluminate of words of your ideas
N   amely to say only one of its kind
N   ativity a story from your mind
E   levate souls to one and all
R   eplenish thoughts to write poems more.

Laird P Brewer

UNEMPLOYED

As if in living death, his figure seems to haunt
The house when she has gone, like the spectre
Of an old man, aged too quickly for his hair to grey
Or wrinkles add a wisdom to his face. Staring out
The window at the ghosts of days that have become
His life, like retirement some thirty years too soon;
Lonely as a pensioner waiting for a different death
To tap him on the shoulder and end this solitude.
In the hourglass of his mind, sands of minutes fall
Slowly and days rest heavy on his once active brain.
Instead of dreaming of the time when she returns
From work he feels the coming autumn closing in
And feels in harmony with season, still no reason
To feel the spring within his youth, in truth
He coils within himself, looking to horizon for rescue
From his vacant situation on time's shelf; wiping
Away a mist of breath that tells him he's still alive
He waits for a new tomorrow to lie to him again.

Derek J Pluck

PIRATES

Pirates used to sail along the seas
Doing as they pleased
They invaded many other ships for treasure
And found counting what they'd gained a pleasure

The Jolly Roger was often hoisted in the daylight
Which brought to many passing ships a fright
Much theft took place
Which was a great disgrace

On pirate ships the captives were killed quite frank
Some were made to walk the plank
At which the pirates enjoyed and laughed
Though it was so horrible and daft

Pirates buried things on many far-off islands
What they'd had a cheek to thieve
With the plan to return there one day
To regain what they'd attacked ships to achieve

To these pirates, thank goodness, there finally came an end
The trouble at sea to deeply descend
When the Navy's tracking was found
And the catching and avoiding of them bound

Today there still may be some treasure islands
Of which no one knows
But to which someone someday goes
And feel out of their mind
With what they find.

Paul Wilkins

MY BABY BROTHER

My baby brother cries all night.
The faces he pulls are a terrible sight.
'He's probably hungry,' my mum said.
How can he be hungry when it's time for bed?
He looks like Grandad, bald with no teeth.
My mum and dad have called him Keith.
His bedroom is blue (the colour for boys!).
And it's filled with cars and cuddly toys.

I like him really, he's tiny and sweet
From the top of his head to his little feet.
I can't wait until he can talk,
Because then we can play and go for a walk.
I'm glad Mum and Dad got him for me.
We'll be the best of friends, just wait and see.

Ann Mandzuk

BOOTS

Beneath the boughs of an almond tree
a soldier stumbles, slumps to a halt
on a crimson-coloured day
shrunk in the chilling knowledge.

It's the boots
that make it difficult.
Bloodied. Muddied.
Repulsive cesspits.
Not the ruptured hearts
battered brains
mangled men forms
mingled with bullets and blossom.

Not wanting to become
a soft-footed phantom
his mind checks the disembodied images
faded in the cruelty of being absent.
His willingness to move
not yet composed
he lingers until the last flower
that will fall has fallen.

It's the boots
that make it difficult.
War begins. You march into it.
War finishes. Then you should return
on a crimson-coloured day
but the boots make it difficult.

Maureen Bold

SADNESS GOES

(Reaction to the rudeness of a lady driver in Anchorsholme)

When you hack at my soul, Cruel World
Thrust the smoking dagger into my heart
Wring my life's blood from enfeebled frame
Hurricane blow!

When you break me on the wheel of life
Watch hot blood drip onto cooling earth
Rip my still beating heart from my breast
Fall driving snow!

When the sun has set in crimson sky
Eyes that close, never more to open
Limbs that stiffen, never more to move
Grim Reaper, Mow!

What's this game of life where never win?
Sunlight always turns to darkened shade
Warmth of summer turns to winter's chill
Shriek carrion crow!

Feel the warmth of sunshine on your neck
Hear the bird, the croaking frog at dawn
Watch the flower blooming, a new-born lamb
All sadness, Go!

David Arran

FEELINGS

Accept my blessings, love and life
Keep them safe deep within your heart
As I know that you have always done,
For my heart too, is full of treasured memories

For it comforts me ever so much,
Knowing that our life together were so beautifully bonded
But sadly had to end so painfully
For life ends, just as well as it starts

But throughout our time together
Not a day has gone past without a tear in my eye,
But they are hidden from you so undisclosed
For that's a thing, I cannot hide even from you,

For you know me all too well, when pain is present
And I am aware that you share a tear in secret
Knowing that I am losing a great battle for that
My last words are, 'I thank you for a wonderful marriage'

And if you hear my voice sometimes
Then you will not forget me after I'm gone
Think of my voice, and I'll be there,
But if you want to cry a little, then that's okay.

S J Davidson

EYES OF THE SLEEPERS

In breathing rooms
Their marshmallow heads
In pillowed sleep,
Submerged in sheeted dreams,
Their eyelids flicker
In rapid eye movements,
What can they see
With their sleeping eyes?

The mind at rest
Is like a tape recorder,
Picking up every impression
Rewinding and replaying at great speed.
Both abstract and concrete
The imagined and the real,
Scrambled egg images
Salt and pepper spiced up dreams.

In some dark recess
They see some other aspect
Another side to themselves,
The unknown is now revealed.
Secret wishes, unspoken desires
Rise to the surface
Of the sleeping sea,
Like sunken continents discovered again.

Come and see
Behind the eyes of the sleepers
Their closed eyes seeing all.
Listen to the hush
Of night's slowly rolling streams
Diving deeper into white
Dream feathers floating
Blown on the wind of dreams.

Ian Barton

SHARING FOOTSTEPS

Desolate landscapes
Growing emptiness
As cold as blue
Surround on abyss
Of cloud and rain
That meet in storms I cry
Yet here I'm never
Held so long
As my cries you shoulder
When tears I bear
The flip side of sadness
Brings with it a smile
Abandoning my fall I stand
Defying gravity's descent
And rising to heights
Where dwell stars and
Promise of horizons both
Clear and new.

A pillar of strength
With whom my life I share
Setting sail on seas of chance
And walking with me throughout
My sleep
You're there for me to catch
My fall
A friend through life
This friend
My wife.

Jason Glennon

'DREAMLAND' BUS 2 EVN STAND

Take this bus to Dreamland
No fear of what waits there.
Make an effort, step inside
You don't need any fare.

Behind his wheel the driver sits
Grinning from ear to ear.
Brush the cobwebs from his door
Let him know you're here.

Sit down at a window seat,
Watch as scenes pass by.
If he drives down Memory Lane
It'll only make you sigh.

This bus ride is through Mind Land
Slough and utter despair.
Feel love's passion and its pain
Your man is waiting there.

He left you on an early bus
The choice it wasn't his.
You kissed him fondly on cold lips
Whilst angels paid his fare.

Dawn lights waken the morning sky
Another day breaks clear.
Brings you closer to the heart
Of one that you hold dear.

Life's journey once begun
Through its laughter, joy and tears.
Cry 'Stop the bus, my dream is done
The terminus is here!'

Francis B Rylance

RIDING THE CIRCLING GLOBE

A ticket to ride caught not bought
    floated from things dimly
like furled wings now opened
    all things seen less grimly

whilst others must act, must do, now
    acting out dynamic
for others reflection and fact
    introjection can sink

not realised this simple truth
    dreaded comfort zone - smashed
butterflies unable to fly
    key needs - everyone's - crashed

training for trainers reach all pits
    learnt - knew - from whence I came
insight seen and needs of others
    not just me - know no blame!

Reflective task - what's helped - up front?
    Life's renewal too much?
What's not helpful is oh so clear
    hiding away's no crutch.

Robert D Shooter

DADDY

Your treasured smiles and loving ways
Will stay with us for all our days.
Your understanding and honest heart
Has been in our lives, a special part.
You lived your life so straight and true
And we are all very proud of you.
You've slipped quietly away to perfect rest
So, all our love, Daddy, goodnight, God bless.

Sandra Thompson

OUT IN THE MEADOW

Oh! I wish I was out in the meadow today,
Cutting the grass, or making the hay,
On a really hot late spring day.

High up above the skylark flutters,
Hoping we'll miss its nest below.
As we are moving to and fro,
Making the swaths, the horses and me,
Out in the meadow, we are all free.

The country sounds, they all are there,
The moles desert their homes in despair.
The clattering machine cuts through their hills,
I hope it is still running free,
Out in the meadow, the horses and me.

Then there comes a familiar shout,
A drink and a bite, there is no doubt.
Out in the meadow in days gone by,
Clean fresh air, and a clear blue sky.

Peter Isles Orr

THE STREET WHERE I WAS BORN

See the streets of this old town
And wonder why they're so old and
Dying now, wrinkled doors and
Numbers falling down,
And children crying for you.
And what's become of Mrs Thompson, Number Two?

I was born and raised in this old
Part of town, my dirty face is
Seen in broken windowpanes.
Hey, Number Ten,
Where Mr Kelly mourned
Death to his first born,
Is tattered and torn and fading now,
And Rosie Clements' penthouse den of
Ill repute is gone -
It was number one to the crew
And what's become of Mrs Thompson, Number Two?

Dustbins, toy balloons and broken skipping ropes
Still litter dusty sidewalks and the road.
The old ice cream place down the alleyway's no longer there;
It's melted to the air forever now.

Mother's calling out the window, time to go to bed
Rest my weary head, forget it all,
Call for Tony nine o'clock, see if he's okay,
'Can he come out to play, Mrs Jones?'

O let me take you home, time to get away from here,
But shed a little tear before we go.

All the people I remember as a golden age,
A lifetime in a cage for wanting you.
And what's become of Mrs Thompson who lived just down the road
at Number Two?

Ron Strickland

REQUIEM

I heard a roll of thunder
That blew my mind asunder
A voice called out my number
On the last day of my life.

Lightning pierced my vision
Images in collision,
That danced in wild derision
In the shadows of my life.

I smelled the stench of hatred
As bomb blast clouds abated
That turned my lungs to paper
One September in my life.

Glass splintered all around me.
Girders crushed and ground me
Timbers warped and bound me
And bled me of my life

I didn't kiss my lover
I didn't hug my brother
I didn't thank my parents
For their precious gift of life.

I pray for peace in this land
I pray for peace in *their* land
I place myself in God's hand
And bless him for my life.

Hayes Turner

BETRAYED

Betrayed and destroyed
By the man I loved
Lied to and abandoned
Pushed and shoved.
What have I done wrong?
I'm bewildered, confused.
I'm mentally tortured
And continually abused.

You left me for another woman
You say this is a lie.
But the truth's in your actions
You are with her, I cry!
You care for her
More than you care for me.
You have destroyed your family
In your desire to be free.

You have used us all
Badly, in this sordid tale.
You think you can win
But I know you will fail.
Your family and friends
Are numb with the news;
Of your callous and selfish
Objectives and views.
Your children and grandchildren
Are suffering too
So for as long as I live
I will not forgive you.

Valerie Cook

GROWING OLD

If as some people say
Age is only in the mind
I wonder why it is then
There's so many things I find
Like for instance having to wear
A bandage on my knee
Not all imagination surely
The thing that comes to me
Off I set to tackle
Something with great zest
Only to find halfway through
I have to stop and rest.

Have those hills grown steeper
The ones I try to climb?
Or is it an indication
Of the passing of time?
As memories of long ago
Seem clearer by the day.
I often stop and wonder
Why I've gone a certain way
Age only in the mind?
Words to encourage me and you
As we inevitably grow old
Sadly it isn't true.

Bill Armstrong

LEADERSHIP

Coal mines dark and dangerous kept proud men in work
many communities depended on those holes in the ground,
Schools, shops and pubs all flourished, then concrete filled each shaft
its wanton destruction, another jewel plucked from our
industrial crown.

Gutsy trawlers lie idle, decommissioned no longer in use
smashed and leaking, reminders of a weak politician's wish,
Leaving captains and deckhands redundant, confused,
shopping at Asda with us for their fish.

An old cleaner in a basement somewhere in Brussels
bashing a typewriter, the long words are a tussle.
Directives by the thousand he drafts to each sector,
ignored by all, except Britain, who hire more inspectors.

Privatisation of industry utilities and power
meant the trains ran on time and our bills all got lowered,
Hospitals and schools are taken over by experts
who say waiting on trolleys in corridors won't hurt.

Its alphabetic destruction of our natural resources
after fish there was farming, chickens, pigs, cows and horses.
Salmonella, BSE and then foot and mouth
a stink of death and corruption seeping in from the south.

T Bates

OUR HOUR OF NEED

Noah found grace in the eyes of the Lord
For Noah loved God and obeyed His word.
The Lord said to Noah:
'Listen to me -
I will flood the land into a mighty sea
and all will perish - except your family -
The beasts of the field, and the fowl of the tree -
will come to you two by two.
I will watch over you until the land is cleansed.
This is my decree,
- for man has turned his face from me.
You will build an ark that will house you all;
it will be wide and deep, long and tall,
and will carry you through the flood that I bring.'
Noah and his sons built that boat
and the beasts came in.
Those who were steeped in sin
laughed and scorned, as Noah warned . .
'The land will flood and you will die!'
'Die!' they cried, 'There's not a cloud in the sky!'
But the rain came . . .
The world changes and fashions are transient.
'Father we have fallen far behind.
Forgive us! This is our hour of need.
Lord, draw us back to you,
we humbly plead.'

Amen.

Bunty Hardman

TRANQUILLITY WAS ETCHED ON MY SOUL

The disease raged,
Silently, through my body.
Twisting and turning,
Thrusting itself through my weakened form.

As a mute plague it stole upon me,
Showing no mercy.
I felt not the fingers of death,
Tightening their grip.

My fragility was exposed
And the malignancy witnessed a window of opportunity.
Moving with rapidity
The remorseless bitterness spread.

My fate was sealed
And the final page was written.
Penned unseen by God's angels,
Their delicate script never fades.

The final curtain suffocated my physical form,
Shrouding me with its density.
Its darkness comforted me.
Providing me with solace.

Celestial movement then drew back the veil,
Revealing the radiance of Heaven.
Peace enveloped me
And drew me to her breast.

My heart revelled
With the knowledge of familiar surroundings.
Secure in the bosom of a loving God,
Tranquillity was etched on my soul.

Valerie Caine

ALIVE

I am beginning to think,
I am beginning to understand,
I am beginning to be!

Light and darkness drift before my eyes,
And cold and warmth my senses stir to feel.
To suckle brings hard work but then reward,
As mother's milk provides my every meal.

I breathe, I sleep, I cry with constant regularity - for why?
This is the rhythm of my life -
A rhythm set by instinct long ago.
And as I grow, delights and pains will shape each subtle change.
No more the blurs of black and white -
Now crystal strands will 'luminate my soul.
I am here; I am alive!

Dorothy Bentley Smith